THE ADEPTS

In the Western Esoteric Tradition

By **MANLY PALMER HALL**

ORDERS OF THE QUEST

ILLUSTRATED

Martino Publishing
Mansfield Centre, CT
2013

Martino Publishing
P.O. Box 373,
Mansfield Centre, CT 06250 USA

ISBN 978-1-61427-485-8

© *2013 Martino Publishing*

Cover design by T. Matarazzo

Printed in the United States of America On 100% Acid-Free Paper

THE ADEPTS

In the Western Esoteric Tradition

By **MANLY PALMER HALL**

ORDERS OF THE QUEST

ILLUSTRATED

PHILOSOPHICAL RESEARCH SOCIETY, Inc.
3341 GRIFFITH PARK BLVD., LOS ANGELES 27, CALIF.

ORDERS OF THE QUEST

In this outline of the adept tradition as it has descended through the mystical Associations and Fraternities of Europe, we are developing our subject material according to a definite plan. The details and particulars will have fuller meaning if the underlying principles are first appreciated. The present section deals with the period extending from the collapse of the pagan Mysteries to the end of the Age of Chivalry. For practical purposes, the Esoteric Schools, which championed the human cause through the Dark Ages and the medieval world, may be considered together as the Orders of the Quest.

The symbolism and rituals of these Fraternities of the Middle Ages involved a search for something remote or hidden. To succeed in the Quest, the knight or companion (disciple) must dedicate himself to the service of his afflicted and exploited fellow man. He must rescue his own soul—the "fair maiden in distress"—by over-coming the giants, dragons, demons, and wicked nobles who pillaged the countryside. As a reward for these noble pursuits, the Christian and godly knight could aspire to a heavenly vision of spiritual mysteries.

The legends of chivalry are veiled accounts of man's eternal search for truth. These beautiful stories are not, however, merely folklore. They are parts of an orderly tradition, unfolding through the centuries and bearing witness to a well-organized plan and program. Like the myths of classical antiquity, the hero tales are sacred rituals belonging to secret Fraternities perpetuating the esoteric doctrines of antiquity.

An attempt to trace the descent of the adept tradition through these centuries of almost complete secrecy is exceedingly difficult. The initiates could not reveal their true identities, their places of habitation, or the programs they were seeking to advance. Most names which have descended to us are pseudonyms, the locations imaginary or deliberately falsified, and the projects themselves concealed under extravagant fables. Unless the student has some sympathetic grasp of the situation and has trained himself to observe landmarks, he can discover little of genuine significance.

It has seemed advisable, however, to approach the subject in a sober and factual manner. We have purposely avoided such reports and accounts as depend entirely upon extrasensory perception for their validity. We are fully aware of the so-called "clairvoyant investigations" and "secret histories" which are preserved and taught by modern mystical sects. It does not seem necessary to our purpose to either accept or reject these traditions, although their inclusion certainly would add glamour to the narration.

The adept tradition in early Europe is traceable by natural means and normal faculties, if we are prepared to undertake the task and have access to the necessary reference material. It is quite possible to overlook or undervalue obscure details, but these do not impair, certainly they do not discredit, the major premise. There is an incontrovertible mass of evidence indicating the existence of initiated philosophers possessing a superior knowledge of divine and natural laws. There is also sufficient proof that these initiates were the agents of a World Fraternity or Brotherhood of Adepts that has existed from the most remote time. This overfraternity has been called the Philosophic Empire, the Great School, the College of the Holy Spirit, and the

Invisible Government of the World. References to this sovereign body of "the ancient ones of the earth" occur in the sacred writings, the philosophical literature, and the mystical traditions of all the races and nations of mankind.

We have selected from the most reputable sources vestiges relating to the Academy of the Adepts. The reader is invited to consider these fragments, to examine their contents, and to discover for himself the veritable accounts which they conceal. We believe that the thoughtful and discriminating student will have little difficulty in recognizing the essential landmarks. We further believe that he will come to understand why we have referred to the stream of the secret doctrine as Humanism. The term is not used in its popular sense, but to describe the grand program of the Mystery Schools for the emancipation of man from bondage to ignorance, superstiton, and fear.

Civilization is unfolding according to a predetermined plan, and not by accident and fortuitous circumstance. This plan does not limit the individual to any creed or doctrine, but invites him to recognize those essential disciplines by which he can attain internal security for himself and can contribute to the final emancipation of all men. The adepts are the philosophic-elect—the priest-kings and the shepherds of the herds of human souls. During enlightened ages, they have appeared as venerated teachers, social reformers, seers, and prophets. In benighted times, their leadership has taken on various appearances, but its substance is unchanging and unchangeable. We have distinguished three important divisions in the European descent of the Mysteries: first, the *Orders of the Quest;* second, the *Orders of the Great Work,* and third, the *Orders of Universal Reformation.* The first group was dedicated to the restoration of the secret sciences through search and discovery. The second group was devoted to the proof and personal accomplishment of that which was known to be true. And the third group was resolved to apply the proven principles of the esoteric tradition to the enlargement, restoration, and reformation of collective society.

If the reader may wonder why we do not attempt to reveal the names, lives, and particular accomplishments of the Masters of the Quest, in this way supplying glamorous biographies of real or suspected adepts of the period, let him pause for a moment and consider. These initiates neither required nor desired the aggrandizement of their persons. Like all worthy men and women, they preferred to be honored through their work, and submerged their identities in their programs so completely that their personalities have become one with their principles. Such biographical material as is available is nearly always mythical and symbolical. What we take to be an account of the men themselves is merely the record of their advancement in the sacred Orders.

In later centuries we have some details about the initiates; but during the period of the Quest, we do well, indeed, if we can identify certain outstanding Humanists with the Secret Societies, which were the proper custodians of the great descent. Our purpose is accomplished if we can convey some general realization of the motions of the Philosophic Empire, from the complete secrecy of its origin to its final emergence as the natural government of the world.

MANLY PALMER HALL

Los Angeles, California; March 1949.

THE ADEPTS

ORDERS OF THE QUEST

The Sons of the Widow

In the 3rd century after Christ, a Persian mystic, born in the faith of Zoroaster and inspired by the doctrines of the Chaldeans, preached a religious philosophy which was to influence the entire course of Western civilization. Manes, or Mani, proclaimed himself the Paraclete, the Comforter promised by Christ to his disciples. The true name of this Persian sage was Shuraik (in Latin, Cubricus), but after his initiation he took the name Manes, which, according to Plutarch, means The Anointed.

Manes, the founder of the Manichaean sect, was born in Babylon, A. D. 215-16. He received his early education from his father, a devoutly religious man, whose spiritual convictions were influenced by Mandaean, Gnostic, and Christian associations. There are also indications that both father and son had a familiarity with the teachings of Sabianism. Later, Manes traveled extensively, was a voluminous writer, and a profound student of the religions of Transoxiana, India, and Western China.*

Manes was an initiate of the Mysteries of Mithras, and among his teachers was Terebinthus, an Egyptian philosopher and magician. There is a tradition that Manes was

* See *Faiths of Man,* by Major General J. G. R. Forlong.

9

at one time a Christian, but this the Church has emphatically denied. It is certain, however, that he contacted early heretical sects, and was also cognizant of the cabalistical speculations of the Jewish mystics. He regarded the philosophical systems of the pagan sages as superior to both Judaism and primitive Christianity. He proclaimed his own ministry at the court of the Persian King, Shapur I, (A. D. 240-42), possibly on the coronation day of that monarch.

The career of the prophet Manes made many demands upon his courage and devotion, but he faced the disasters of his life sustained by internal visions and mystical experiences. He was unable to maintain a favorable position in the Persian court due to the pressure exerted against him by the priests of Zoroaster. He acquired some distinction as a physician, but his skill was not sufficient to preserve the life of one of the sons of the ruling prince. His prestige undermined, Manes was exiled through the contrivances of the Mazdians, and he undertook his memorable journeys. During this same period, he lived for a year in a cave, with only wild herbs for food.

Later, Manes was recalled to Persia by a more generous prince, was received with great honors, and a palace was erected for his use. For a brief time his fortunes flourished, and he was consulted on important matters of state. But when Bahram I ascended the throne, the prophet fell upon evil times. Bahram, for political reasons, supported the Zoroastrian clergy, and these were resolved to destroy the heretical sect and its founder. Manes was crucified and flayed alive (A. D. 276-77), and his body was exposed to various indignities.

The doctrine of Manes was rooted in Persian dualism, but he drew essential dogmas from the various schools of

Southern Europe, Mesopotamia, North Africa, and Central Asia. The Manichaeans practiced the sacraments of baptism and communion. They accepted the ministry of Christ, but not the divinity of Jesus. Manes condemned the Christians as worshipers of idols, declaring that they had substituted men for gods, and then images for men. The sect, however, admired St. Paul, and acknowledged *Jesus Impatibalis,* the Christ within that was the hope of glory.

After the death of Manes, the progress of the sect was entrusted to a circle of initiates, and these defined the degrees of the Order, its initiatory rites, signs, symbols, and passwords. The broad esoteric foundation of Manichaeism appealed to scholars of all beliefs, including the better-informed Christians. Salomon Reinach gives the following valuable summary of the history of the sect: "The Manichaeans were gentle and peaceable persons; this was the opinion of the Greek philosopher Libanius. But as they rejected the rites of existing Churches, and claimed to confine themselves to the ministrations of their own priests, those of other religions persecuted them furiously, and excited the mob against them by calumnies. When it was first attacked in Persia, Manicheeism spread toward Turkistan, India and China, and at the same time towards Africa by way of Syria and Egypt. Diocletian prohibited it in A. D. 290, and the Christian Emperors from A. D. 377 onward legislated against it; the Vandals burnt or exiled the Manichaeans. African Manicheeism is known to us chiefly through the works of St. Augustine, who wrote long treatises against its doctors, after having been their pupil. In the east, the sect was almost exterminated by the severity of Justinian, but it formed again in Asia Minor. We read of the *Paulitians* in Armenia (seventh to twelfth centuries), the *Bogomiles* in Thrace (tenth to eleventh century). The

Byzantine Emperors, Alexis Comnenus in particular, pursued these inoffensive sectaries with fire and sword. In the eleventh century Manicheeism, brought by the commerce of the Levant, penetrated into Southern France, and gave rise to the powerful sect of the *Cathari,* who were ex-terminated by the Inquisition."*

Heckethorn extends this history with many interesting details. He notes: "By changing its name, seat, and figurative language, Manichaeism spread in Bulgaria, Lombardy (Patarini), France (Cathari, Albigenses), etc., united with the Saracens, and openly made war upon the Emperor, and its followers perished by thousands in battle and at the stake; and from its secular trunk sprang the so-called heresies of the Hussites and Wyckiffites, which opened the way for Protestantism."†

The same author then establishes the Templars and Freemasons in the Manichaean descent, and concludes by showing how their doctrines were echoed in the songs of the Troubadours and the covenants of the guilds. From the Societies, Fraternities, and Orders which perpetuated the esoteric doctrine of the Manichaeans, we gain considerable insight into the essential teachings of the sect. They believed in a primitive religion ever-existing in the world, of which formal theologies were corrupted forms. They held that enlightened and purified love was the highest of human emotions, and manifested as a simple and natural love for God in heaven above and for man on the earth below.

The practical religion of love was expressed through kindliness, friendliness, tolerance, and patience. The wise man became the protector or father of those less informed than himself. Only those who truly loved their fellow men

---

*See *Orpheus, a History of Religions.*
†See *Secret Societies of All Ages.*

and proved that affection through the defense of the rights of man were entitled to regard themselves as religious. The secret assemblage of the Manichaeans was dedicated to the liberation of the human being from all despotism and tyranny. The end to be attained was an enduring brotherhood of mankind. Men should be ruled by love alone and should love their rulers. Leaders should deserve this affection, and all kingdoms and nations should dwell together in peace, governed by just laws and noble examples. All tyranny must end; all false doctrines must fall when the light of truth—the Christ within—is acknowledged as the Universal Redeemer.

St. Augustine was drawn to Manichaeism because it interpreted the Christian religion in terms acceptable to his inquiring mind. He had already decided that the Church was ridden with superstition and lacked philosophic depth. He remained absorbed in this so-called heresy for nine years, but was never able to penetrate deeply enough into the mysticism of the sect to overlook the shortcomings of the members. Certainly his subsequent opinions were influenced by his associations with the followers of Manes. He departed from them through a disinterest in mysticism, for which his intellect was not suited.

The Church, in the treatment of the Manichaeans, followed its usual procedure of accusing all heretical groups of practicing immoral and infernal rites. St. Augustine, who had an intimate knowledge of the sect, made no such accusations. His temperament would have inclined him to do so had there been any reasonable grounds. After departing from the heresy of Manes, St. Augustine came under the influence of Bishop Ambrose, a fine and noble man addicted to the teachings of Origen. Origen now stands precariously on the borderline of heresy, for he himself was influenced by Gnosticism, Neoplatonism, and, incredible as it may seem, by the doctrine of Manes.

Some of the writings of Manes have survived, and from them we learn their concept of the Divine Nature: "The spirit of God is Light, radiant with the virtue of love, faith, fidelity, high-mindedness, wisdom, meekness, knowledge, understanding, mystery, and insight." Leo the Great decided that such a belief should be stamped out lest the creed of the Church be extinguished. This pontiff also found it embarrassing to contemplate the idea that in the spiritual succession Jesus was succeeded by Manes, who was the last and greatest of the prophets emanated from the Divine, and who was the ambassador of the Light of the World.

One of the annual rituals of the Manichaeans was celebrated to commemorate the crucifixion of the prophet. This consisted of placing a chair on a platform with five steps. Those members of the Order who had purified themselves for the occasion were permitted to kneel before this empty chair which symbolized the "unseen Master" of their sect. This empty chair is reminiscent of the vacant throne of Osiris, in the Egyptian initatory ritual. The followers of Manes were called "the Sons of the Widow" and the founder himself was referred to as "the Widow's Son." The popular story that Manes gained this title by being redeemed from slavery by a rich widow is about as plausible as the legend that the Order of the Garter was created in honor of the Countess of Salisbury's garter.

Horus, the savior-god of the Osirian mysteries of Egypt, was a "Widow's Son." He was posthumously conceived by the holy spirit of Osiris, his murdered father. The ghost of Osiris overshadowed his sister-wife, Isis, who had dressed herself in widow's weeds to lament her dead husband. Horus, thus strangely and immaculately conceived, was destined to become the "hero of the world" and the avenger of his father. In fact, it was believed by some that Horus was possessed by the spirit of his own father. The hieroglyphic of Osiris is the All-seeing-Eye combined with the Empty Throne. Isis is the Virgin of the World, who bears the divine child without the loss of her virginity. She is the esoteric tradition which gives birth to the adepts by a mystery "in the spirit." She is the Sophia of the Gnosis, the "blessed demoiselle" of the Troubadours and the later mystics. In Christian and neo-Christian symbolism, Sophia appears again as the "Bride of the Lamb."

Manes, therefore, was not literally a widow's son, for his father survived to assist in his education. He had attained the second birth; that is, he had been born out of the womb of the Mysteries, and those of his followers who had received the initiation were identified in the same way. By his martyrdom Manes became another Osiris, Lord of the Empty Throne. He overshadowed his Order as a spirit, and from the sanctuary of Manes were born new sons to extend his doctrines, thus becoming in a mystical sense the re-embodiment of himself. Deprived of their Master, the body of the Manichaeans was appropriately symbolized by the legend of Isis mourning for her martyred Lord.

The Albigenses.

In order to appreciate the degree of organized resistance that developed in Europe against the remnants of the pagan philosophical schools, it is only necessary to consider the fate of the Albigensian heretics. The sect originated in Manichaeism, a school of esoteric philosophy which exercised a considerable influence over the early life of St. Augustine. Later this pious man devoted much time and many words to a bitter denunciation of the heresiarch Manes. It is probable that the Albigenses originated in

Bulgaria, but their principal stronghold was in Southern France, where they created a considerable stir during the 12th and 13th centuries.

So thoroughly were the Albigensian doctrines stamped out by the Roman Church that it is almost impossible to restore the structure of their beliefs. We know that they were Catharists believing in the ultimate salvation of all men. They were devout Christians but rejected the machinery of the Church, and taught that any who died without being reconciled to God through the mystery of Christ would be born again in the physical world as a human being or an animal. The Catharists baptized by the laying on of hands, and taught that the kingdom of Christ was a mystery of the spirit and not of this world.

The Albigenses also derived inspiration from the Bogomiles, a religious community of considerable antiquity which inspired many of the unorthodox sects of Russia. The Bogomiles denied the miraculous birth of Christ, rejected most of the sacraments of the Church, baptized only adults, had no formal places of worship, and interpreted the miracles of Jesus mystically rather than literally. They had the quaint notion that Satan was responsible for setting up all the churches of Christendom as a means of destroying human souls.

It is quite understandable that in 1209 Pope Innocent III obliged the Cistercians to preach a crusade against the Albigensian heretics. In the civil war that followed, the Provencal civilization was destroyed, but the Albigenses survived. About thirty years later the Inquisition stepped in with better success.

Maurice Magre writes of the Albigenses thus: "I feel indignant at a great injustice which has never been remedied and seems unlikely to be remedied. Those self-controlled unassuming men who lived in Southern France during the 13th century, whose practical rule was poverty and whose ideal was love of their fellowmen, were exterminated, and calumny has triumphantly wiped out even their name and their memory. Calumny has been so active and so skillful that the descendants of these wonderful men are unaware of the noble history of their ancestors, and when they wish to learn it, it is presented in such a fashion that they blush at their extraordinary past."*

It seems that some of the Catharist communities practiced a mode of life strongly reminiscent of the Syrian Essenes. C. W. Heckethorn gives us an excellent summary of their doctrine and conduct: "In spite of the Church many Italian cities including Milan, Florence, Naples, and even Rome itself were centers of Cathari activity. A Cathari concealed its doctrine from all but its higher initiates. It taught metempsychosis assuming that to attain the light seven such transmigrations were required. This however may possibly refer to the degrees of their initiation. They rejected the Old Testament account of the creation, and had communistic tendencies; were adverse to marriage; were philanthropists; they lived industrious lives, combining saving habits with charity; founded schools and hospitals. . . . They performed their ceremonies in forests, caverns and remote valleys. At his initiation the novice received a garment made of fine linen and wool which he wore under his shirt. The women received a girdle which they wore next to the skin above the waist."†

The same author describes the fate of Dolcino, one of the leaders of the Italian Catharists. He and his wife Margaret were pursued by the Inquisition in 1307. They were captured and torn to pieces, limb by limb, and the

---

*See *Magicians, Seers, and Mystics*.
†See *Secret Societies of All Ages and Countries* (London, 1897).

pieces afterwards burned by the public executioner. Fifteen years later, thirty of Dolcino's disciples were burned alive in the market place at Padua. The remnants of these so-called heretical movements found some refuge in Eastern Europe in areas which came under the political domination of the Turks.

Under the general name Albigenses, these several schools of primitive and mystical Christianity bestowed their life and vitality upon the Knights Templars, the Rosicrucians, and later, by descent, upon the Bavarian Illuminists. The Crusaders brought back to Europe the Eastern Manichaeism with its rationalizing and moderating influences. Reforms long overdue began to stir beneath the surface of the medieval world. As one writer has expressed it: "Philosophy, republicanism, and industry assailed the Holy See."

It is known that the inner council of the Albigenses consisted of initiates whose method of development was not dissimilar to that of the Gnostics or the Neoplatonists. These initiates were internally enlightened men, dedicated to the perpetuation of Plato's concepts of the Philosophic Empire and the philosopher-king. Only those who lived the Christian life could know the Christian doctrine. By the end of the 14th century the sect disappeared entirely, and such physical power as it may have been said to enjoy was entirely destroyed. This so-called power was simply an appeal to virtue, and at no time did the sect exhibit any physical ambitions other than those of justice, charity, and humility.

It is certain that the adepts of the Albigenses, Catharists, and Bogomiles did not perish with the fall of their schools. Such a sacrifice would have accomplished nothing of practical benefit to mankind. They chose to remain hidden and to create new channels for the dissemination of their doctrines. These channels changed their appearances to meet the requirements of time and place. Thus, there is no break in the esoteric descent of essential truths even though the physical institutions were destroyed by the fanaticism and cruelty of an unbelieving world.

The Glory of the Guilds

It is now fairly well-established that the art of papermaking was brought to Europe from the Near East by the Crusaders returning from the Holy Land, or by the Moors who established their culture in Spain. Indications seem to point to China as the country responsible for the invention of paper. Harold Bayley opens a large subject when he writes: "It is a fact, the significance of which has hitherto been unnoticed, that the early papermaking districts were precisely those that were strongholds of the heretical sects known as the Albigenses. The word 'Albigenses' is a term applied loosely to the various pre-Reformation reformers whose stronghold stretched from Northern Spain across the southern provinces of France from Lombardy to Tuscany."*

Papermaking opened the way for printing in Europe. Printing from movable type also was invented in China or Korea at least two hundred years before its appearance in Europe. The histories of European papermaking and printing are exceedingly vague. Almost nothing is known of the circumstances leading to the production of books in the West. Bayley made an extensive study of the watermarks, head pieces, and colophons appearing in early books. He is convinced that these indicate the existence of a secret religious tradition or spiritual communion by which these artisans constituted an esoteric Fraternity or Brotherhood.

*See *A New Light on the Renaissance.*

The persecution of the Albigenses scattered the Masters of the sect over the entire Continent. The higher initiates of the Albigenses were called the Perfect Ones; and, according to one writer, in the year A.D. 1240 at least four thousand of these Perfect Ones were wandering about Europe in various disguises as troubadours, peddlers, merchants, and journeymen. These artisans and craftsmen established themselves in their chosen crafts and trades, and from them descended many distinguished printing establishments. That these printers were members of a Secret Order explains a situation otherwise completely incredible.

In the great period of the publication of books and tracts dealing with alchemy, cabalism, magic, Rosicrucianism, and the projected reformation of the arts and sciences, an unusual situation arose. Most of the books were published anonymously or under pseudonyms. In many cases elaborate ciphers were incorporated into the text, and curious emblems and symbolical figures were introduced. Such an elaborate program, involving printers in several countries operating with extreme secrecy, would not have been possible without the complete co-operation of the printers themselves. In spite of bribery, threat, and persecution, the printers revealed neither the sources of the manuscripts which they published nor the true names of the authors. If it can be proved, as present indications suggest, that the printers, typesetters, and engravers were themselves citizens of the same Invisible Commonwealth as the authors, philosophers, mystics, and scholars, the dimensions of the project become clearly defined.

Take, for example, the famous "jug" watermark found in the paper on which most of the first editions of the writings of Lord Bacon were printed. This jug recurs also in many of the publications involved in the early Rosicrucian controversy. The jug is a vase or pitcher, sometimes shown

filled with fruit or grapes. Bayley believes that this vase
or pitcher is the Holy Grail. He supports his conviction
with many ingenious examples of this vase which can be
traced directly to the Albigensian papermakers. In my
library is a copy of Burton's *Anatomy of Melancholy* with
the vase watermark. On one leaf only—the dedication
page—appears an entirely different watermark, consisting
of a heart that contains within it a crucified rose. This is
a complete Rosicrucian emblem, and the book itself contains references to the Rosicrucians.

WATERMARK DEVICE
From dedication page of the 1628 edition of *The Anatomy of Melancholy*.

Those who doubt the existence of hidden texts within
certain books of the late 16th and early 17th centuries have
always objected on the grounds that printers would have
to be a party to the secret texts, and could not have been
prevented from exposing the facts in the course of time.
Also, a vast amount of labor which would have been extremely costly would necessarily be involved. If, however,
the printers were performing a labor of love and were themselves initiates of a Secret Order, these objections are no
longer valid.

After the invention of printing, the myths, legends, and
fables of the Troubadours and jongleurs gradually drifted
toward their final published forms. In almost every in-

stance, the so-called authors of these curious works merely
acted as editors or compilers of earlier fictions. The medieval mind was not addicted to fictional literature such as is
popular in the present century. Most works in a lighter
vein were morality fables or else were burdened with social
or political significance. Most of these slighter productions
were tinged with heresy, and perpetuated the Humanism of
the trouveres.

The *Ship of Fools,* first printed in Germany in 1494, is an
early example of a school of satirical writing attacking the
prevailing foibles and follies of the day. Little is known

THE SHIP OF FOOLS
From the enlarged edition published in Paris, 1500.

of Alexander Barclay, who is credited with the authorship
of this outstanding poem. The spirit of the book reflects
an intellectual transition from mental surfdom to that state
of intellectual revolution which made possible the right of
free thought.

Although but little read in these days, the beast-epic,
Reynard the Fox, which originated apparently in France
near the border of Flanders, was one of the most popular

works of folklore.   Harold Bayley writes of this cycle of
animal stories thus: "The stories of how Reynard the Fox
outwitted his traditional enemy, Isengrim the Wolf, were
popular in Europe for many centuries.   If we substitute
Heresy for Reynard, and *Rome* for Isengrim, we can understand why these seemingly childish stories enjoyed such an
immense vogue.   'These Heretic foxes,' percipiently said
Gregory IX, 'have differnt faces, but they all hang together
by the tails.' "   Unfortunately, the French originals of the
stories are lost, but it is safe to assume that they originated
in the 13th century among those same Troubadours who
found so many adroit means of discomfiting the monkish
Orders.

The "Dance of Death" is the name generally given to a
series of pictures and moral compositions intended to re-
mind the thoughtful of the impermanence of material digni-
ties and honors.   The symbolism originated in pagan
antiquity, but the development of the theme is now associated with Swiss artists working in Basel in the late 13th
and early 14th centuries.   This version of *la danse macabre*
is referred to as the Basel recension.

It seems to me that this cycle of morality emblems is
part of the Humanist motion.   All the designs point to
death as the destroyer of the artificial preferments bestowed
by wealth, heredity, and political conspiracy.   The rich and
the poor, the great and the small, the high and the low are
called from their various preoccupations by the drums of
death.   No one is immune, and thus all ambitions are part
of the passing vanity of the world.   The pictures preached
a powerful message against privileged classes, and recommended that the human being dedicate his life to the
accumulation of those spiritual treasures which could not
be taken from him by the capering skeleton.   In death, the
Pope and the peasant, the king and the beggar danced to-

gether to the pipes of the unwelcome musician.

The English legendary hero, Robin Hood, the last of the Saxons, arose in the first half of the 14th century. This bold yeoman is said to have flourished at the time of Richard Coeur de Lion; and as the legends grew, this outlaw became the culture hero of the *bourgeoisie,* as King Arthur was the culture hero of the aristocracy. Robin Hood was an operating Humanist. Not only was he a Saxon against the Normans, but he stole from the rich and

—From *A New Light on the Renaissance*
PRINTER'S ORNAMENT
Representing the Court of Love of the Troubadours, in the form of a walled garden with strange flowers. The mystic rose dominates the design.

gave to the poor. He was devoutly religious, but found immense satisfaction in plaguing plump abbots and pompous clerics of all degrees. He stood for the free life, and was distinctly the "superman" of his day. Here, again, the storytellers preached a gospel of equality and democracy, and strengthened that love of liberty in the hearts of all just men. Maid Marian appears much as in the romances of the Troubadours; and in the development of the Secret Fraternity of the Greenwood, we have a parallel with the Courts of Love and Honor, sung by the minstrels of Brittany and Provence.

Usually the printers included secret marks in their books or engravings to indicate the presence of a cipher or double meaning. Large and intricate initial letters, including curious designs, sometimes served the same purpose. Most of the enigmas and rebuses have never been solved because of the prevailing indifference to the motives behind the motions of history. Even where it is suspected, as in the case of *Gulliver's Travels,* that a satire was intended, it is assumed that the author wrote entirely on his own responsibility according to his own taste. It has not occurred to bibliophiles generally that the writers themselves might be bound into a secret league and be operating according to a formal plan.

We should pause to consider the bookbinders, for these men also belonged to a guild, and were in a position to perpetuate many curious emblems and figures on the covers of books. Unfortunately, bindings are more fragile than the contents of the volumes, and only in museums and very large private collections can the student examine a representative group of original 15th- and 16th-century bookbindings. The traditional designs and ornaments include symbols known to have belonged to the Albigensian cult and the Secret Societies dominating the transitional period in European culture.

As the result of a certain confraternity which included within itself the various trade guilds, other landmarks were left to guide the observing searcher. European public buildings, especially cathedrals, libraries, and tombs, were adorned with innumerable devices in no way parts of the approved designs. Often these embellishments were concealed in obscure places, but scarcely a medieval structure has survived which does not include the symbols and signatures of the Secret Societies. The conspiracy extended through the entire world of the arts. This broad dissemination was only possible because the separate guilds and unions were aware of the high purpose for which the guild system had been established.

The guilds formed a link between the Troubadours and the trade unions. The trade unions were societies of artisans nourished by the apprentice system. The secrets of various arts and crafts were jealously guarded by the guild Masters, whose arms and crests dangled from hooks around the great Guild Cup in the midst of their Lodge. This Guild Cup was again the Chalice of Bacchus, the Holy Grail, and the symbolical Cup of the Mysteries.

The guild Masters used the language of their crafts to conceal the mysticism of the great Humanist Reformation. Each guild taught the Universal Mystery in the language of its own art. Thus, within architectural terms, the stonemasons concealed the building of the universal temple of the brotherhood of man. The guild system took deep roots in Germany, but was also well-established in other countries on the Continent, and in England. So far as the world knew, the guilds were simply trade unions, but there was scarcely one of them which was not influenced to some degree by the old heresy of Manes.

It is difficult to distinguish the details of the transition which resulted in the emergence of the German Minnesingers from the older body of the Bards and the Troubadours. The term *Minnesang* (*minne*, meaning love) was originally applied to the song or poem written by a knight to express his passionate devotion to the mistress of his heart. It was not long, however, before the term took on a wider meaning to include all music and poetry: religious, political, and amorous.

The principles of the Minnesang reached Germany from Provence, which was one of the last strongholds of the Albigensian Troubadours. The kings of Provence were patrons of the arts, and under their protection there was a brief flowering of song and poetry. Most of the Minnesingers were drawn from the ranks of the gentry, and it was only natural that the less-privileged classes should develop their version of the same convictions. Out of the Minnesingers, with their combination of mournful tunes, and also from the music of the peasantry evolved the Meistersingers, the burgher musicians of Germany. For the most part, the Order was composed of artisans, good solid citizens, with long coats, square-toed shoes, and orthodox religious convictions. They were good, practical men, hard-working, shrewd, and skillful in their crafts. Few, if any, had received formal education in music, and their talents were natural rather than acquired.

The long shadow of the Manichaean doctrine reached into the guildhalls and even into the somber cloisters of the cathedrals. The guilds were champions of the human cause, institutions of fair play and honest practice. They were co-operatives, protecting their members from society in general, and protecting society from shoddy goods and unreasonable exploitation. In a quiet way, the guild masters legislated the life of the times, and these solid, good-hearted citizens endeavored in all things to judge righteous judgment. What better place could be found in which to plant the seeds of the democratic dream? From these small centers of self-government might flow the concept of the World Guild, the World Commonwealth, indeed the Philosophic Empire.

The Meistersingers declared their Order to have originated with twelve guild poets, who had derived their
inspiration from the Troubadours and the Minnesingers.
The very selection of this number and its use in their symbolism suggests that the Order originated in the old Mystery systems, which always celebrated twelve gods, twelve
prophets, twelve patriarchs, or twelve disciples. When we
attempt to trace the twelve guild poets of the Middle High
German, we come immediately upon the most celebrated
name associated with the Minnesang, Wolfram von Eschenbach. He competed in the tourney of the poets known as
the Wartsburgskrieg. This episode is preserved for music
lovers in Wagner's opera, *Tannhauser*. The place occupied
by von Eschenbach in the descent of the Orders of the
Quest will be given greater consideration in the sections
devoted to the Grail legends.

The Knights Templars

In *Isis Unveiled*, H. P. Blavatsky refers to the Knights
Templars as "the last European secret organization which,
as a body, had in its possession some of the mysteries of
the East." A few paragraphs later she adds: "They
reverenced the doctrines of alchemy, astrology, magic,
kabalistic talismans, and adhered to the secret teachings
of their chiefs in the East."

The Order of Knights Templars was founded in 1118
by Hugh de Payen and Geoffrey of St. Omer, together with
seven other French knights then stationed in Palestine.
These gentlemen were motivated by a determination to
guard the roads of Christian pilgrimage to the shrine of
the Holy Land. During the first nine years of the Order,
the Templars lived in extreme poverty. Hugh de Payen
and Geoffrey of St. Omer had but one war horse between
them. This circumstance was perpetuated on the great seal

of the Templars, which consisted of two knights seated on one charger. The influence of the Order increased rapidly, for it appealed to the concepts of chivalry which dominated the minds of the time. In 1128 the Council of Troyes graciously acknowledged its motives and principles, and St. Bernard prepared a code for the spiritual and temporal guidance of the knights.

Pope Honorius confirmed the Order of the Temple, and appointed a white mantle as the distinguishing habit. Later Eugenius III added a red cross to be worn affixed to the

SEAL OF THE KNIGHTS TEMPLARS

breast. They also had a banner made of stripes of red and black cloth. The members were bound by severe obligations. They took vows of poverty, ate only the coarsest of foods, and were denied the simplest of pleasures, even those of the hunt. When not warring against the enemies of Christ and the Church, they lived in monastic seclusion in the various houses of retreat which had been assigned to them. Here they divided their attentions between such religious activities as prayer and penace, and such practical concerns as "furbishing their armor and mending their clothes." They were forbidden the common military recrea tion of gambling, and could not even play chess.

Candidates for initiation gave all their property and personal goods to the Order. Thus, while each was individually poor, the body as a whole became enormously rich. The principal officer of the Templars was the Grand Master, and, as the worldly estates of the body increased, he ranked as a prince at all the courts of Europe. Each new member took vows of chastity and obedience. "I swear," said the novice, "to consecrate my thoughts, my energy, and my life, to the defense of the unity of God and the mysteries of the faith. . . . I promise to be submissive and obedient to the Grand Master of the Order."*

Eliphas Levi and several other authors and historians advance the belief that Hugh de Payens had been initiated into a strange sect of Christian Johannites then flourishing in the East. The members of this group claimed that they alone were in possession of the inner mysteries of Christ. The supreme pontiffs of the Johannites assumed the title of "Christ" and claimed an uninterrupted transmission of power from the days of St. John.

Dr. Oliver points out that many Secret Associations of the ancients either flourished or originated in Syria. It was here the Dionysian Artificers, the Essenes, and the Kasideans arose. In a work published in 1855, Dr. Oliver says: "We are assured, that, not withstanding the unfavorable conditions of that province, there exists, at this day, on Mount Libanus, one of these Syriac Fraternities. As the Order of the Templars, therefore, was originally formed in Syria, and

---

*See *Royal Masonic Cyclopaedia*, by Kenneth R. H. Mackenzie.

existed there for a considerable time, it would be no improbable supposition that they received their Masonic knowledge from the Lodges in that quarter.   But we are fortunately in this case not left to conjecture, for we are expressly informed by a foreign author,* who was well acquainted with the history and customs of Syria, that the Knights Templars were actually members of the Syriac Fraternities."†

To understand the forces operating behind the Knights Templars, it is necessary to examine the doctrines of the Johannite Order of Oriental Christians.   They seemed to have derived inspiration from the Nazarenes and certain Gnostic sects that denied the divinity of Christ, but acknowledged Jesus to be a great and holy prophet.   They rejected utterly the Immaculate Conception and other cardinal tenets of the Western Church.   The Johannites claimed to possess ancient records to the effect that when Jesus was a small child he was adopted by a Rabbi named Joseph, who carried him into Egypt where he was initiated into the occult sciences.   The priests of Osiris, regarding him as the long-promised incarnation of Horus expected by the adepts, finally consecrated him Sovereign-Pontiff of the universal religion.

At the time of Hugh de Payen, Theocletes was the living "Christ" of the Johannites.   He communicated to the founders of the Temple the ideas of a sovereign priesthood of dedicated and initiated men united for the purpose of overthrowing the bishops of Rome and the establishment of universal civil liberty.   The secret object of the Johannites was the restoration of the esoteric tradition and the gathering of mankind under the one eternal religion of the world.

---

*Adler in *Drusis Montis Libani* (Rome, 1786).
†See *The History and Illustrations of Freemasonry Compiled From an Ancient Publication* (New York, 1855).

Thus, from the beginning, the knights of the Temple served two doctrines. One was concealed from all except the leaders and certain trusted members; the other, publicly stated and practiced for the sake of appearances, conformed with the regulations of the Church. Although some opponents declared that the Templars were seeking to dominate European civilization and establish their own sovereignty

JACQUE DE MOLAY

The last Grand Master of the Knights Templars

over both Church and State, like the Teutonic Knights of Prussia or the Hospitalers of Malta, these accusations reveal a complete ignorance of the secret philosophy of the Temple. Historians have pointed out that these knights disturbed the kingdom of Palestine by their rivalry with the Hospitalers, concluded leagues with the infidels, made war upon Cyprus and Antiochia, dethroned the king of Jerusalem, Henry II, devastated Greece and Thrace, refused to contribute to the ransom of St. Louis, and declared for

Aragon against Anjou, an unpardonable crime in the eyes of France. Nothing is said, however, of the corruption that flourished among the institutions which the Templars opposed. At worst, they could be guilty only of counter-conspiracy, for Christendom at that time was devoted to a grand conspiracy against the parts of itself.

Jacque de Molay, the last Grand Master of the Temple, was elected in 1297. Historians agree that this French knight was a man of noble character, and conducted himself in an estimable manner throughout the difficult and tragic years of his rulership. Writers with various personal attitudes have advanced several explanations for the circumstances which led to the persecution and destruction of the Order of the Temple. When all the elements of the story have been examined, it appears that their greater crimes were those of being wealthy and powerful. The French king, Philip the Fair, and the Roman Pope, Clement V, were resolved to destroy the Knights Templars and divide the treasures of the Order between themselves.

The persecution of the Templars, thinly veiled under ecclesiastical and secular trials and convictions, extended over a period of approximately six years, and Jacque de Molay was imprisoned five and a half years before his execution. During this time the Grand Master, together with most of his officers and more prominent knights, was subjected to indescribable tortures. Many died of pain and exhaustion, and some, unable to endure further suffering, confessed to the crimes with which they had been charged. A number of these, however, later retracted their confessions and died gallantly, rather than to perjure their immortal souls to preserve their bodies.

Typical of the means employed to destroy the Temple is the manner in which the first charges were made. Two criminals, both former Templars who had been expelled

from the Order for heresy and other offenses, were languish-
ing in prison. These men, to obtain their own liberation,
resolved to accuse the Templars of monstrous offenses
against the Church and State. According to their charges,
the Order denied Christ, the Virgin, and the saints; practiced idolatry, cannibalism, witchcraft, debaucheries, and
abominations. The two miserable men were released from
prison as a reward for their lies, but they gained little from
their liberty. One was afterward hanged, and the other,
beheaded. It was upon such perjured testimony that the
most magnificent Order of Chivalry was reduced to ashes.

De Molay must have realized from the beginning of the
elaborate series of trials that justice had no place in the
procedures. The Order was doomed from the beginning,
and on the 18th of March 1314, he stood before the
cardinal of Alba and heard the sentence of perpetual imprisonment. When the cardinal began a detailed account
of the guilt of the Templars based upon confessions obtained
by torture, the Grand Master interrupted him with a sweep-
ing denial: "I know the punishments which have been
inflicted on all the knights who had the courage to revoke
a similar confession; but the dreadful spectacle which is
presented to me is not able to make me confirm one lie by
another. The life offered to me on such infamous terms
I abandon without regret."

The commissioners were confounded, for they believed
that torture and imprisonment had broken the spirit of the
Templars. Guy, the Grand Preceptor of the Temple, then
spoke echoing the sentiments of the Grand Master. When
King Philip learned the course that events were taking, his
rage knew no bounds, and, without even recourse to the procedure of the ecclesiastical court, he decreed that the
knights should be immediately burned at the stake. The
following day (according to some authorities, late the same

night) the Grand Master and the Grand Preceptor were brought to a small island in the River Seine, opposite the king's garden, and chained to posts, around which had been heaped a quantity of charcoal. The fuel had been arranged to burn slowly, so that the condemned men would suffer the maximum pain and distress.

After the fires had been lighted, de Molay addressed the huge assemblage with these prophetic words: "France will remember our last moments. We die innocent. The decree that condemns us is an unjust decree, but in heaven there is an august tribunal, to which the weak never appeal in vain. To that tribunal, within forty days, I summon the Roman Pontiff. Oh! Philip, my king, I pardon thee in vain, for thy life is condemned at the tribunal of God. Within a year I await thee."

The pontiff was stricken by an obscure ailment and actually died on the 19th day of the following month. The Church in which his body was placed took fire, and the corpse was half consumed. King Philip, before the year had elapsed, also departed from this world in misery and great pain. Most of the active persecutors of the Order perished by premature or violent deaths—events which caused widespread consternation.

There is a legend held by some authorities and rejected by others that in 1314 Jacque de Molay, realizing that his end was near, appointed Johannes Marcus Lormenius to be his successor. It is pointed out that the election of Lormenius can be questioned, because the Order was unable to install him by the usual procedure. But extreme circumstances justified extreme measures, and the charter, bearing the signatures of the proper persons, is said to be still preserved in Paris.

Levi gives a slightly different account. According to him, de Molay organized and instituted Occult Masonry.

"Within the walls of his prison he founded four Metro-politan Lodges—at Naples for the East, Edinburg for the West, Stockholm for the North, and Paris for the South."*
The same author refers to the French Revolution as the daughter of the great Johannite Orient, and the ashes of the Templars.†

Among the accusations against the Templars was that they worshiped a strange and secret god. Deodat Jafet, one of the knights, speaking "of his own free will" after many hours of being broken on the rack, confessed anything that the inquisitors required. Under the gentle inspiration of thumbscrews and an iron boot crushing his heel bones, he described an image supposedly venerated by the Tem-plars: "I was alone in a chamber with the person who received me: he drew out of a box a head, or idol, which appeared to me to have three faces, and said *thou shouldest adore it as thy Saviour and that of the order of the Temple*." Later, Jafet retracted his entire confession, and stood to the last as one of the defenders of the Order.

It is possible that this three-faced image was a Brahman Trimurti, which had come into the possession of the Tem-plars during their years in the Near East, or it may have existed only in the prepared confessions which the knights were so pleasantly induced to sign. In either event, this idol came to be identified with the secret activities of the Societies which perpetuated the Mysteries of the Temple.

It should be mentioned that the knights were also accused of adoring a curious deity in the form of a monstrous head or a demon in the form of a goat. This idol, named Baphomet, the goat of Mendes, has been called the secret god of the Templars. According to Levi, Baphomet should

*See *History of Magic*.
†See *Transcendental Magic*.

be spelled cabalistically backwards, and consists of three abbreviations: TEM. OHP. AB., *Templi omnium hominum pacis abbas* (the father of the temple of universal peace among men).

TITLE PAGE OF ANDREAE'S *MYTHOLOGIAE CHRISTIANAE*
(Strasbourg, 1619)

This figure includes one of the earliest representations of the compass and square, and at the base is the three-faced deity of the Knights Templars.

Although it is a popular belief that the Knights Templars were for the most part unlearned and incapable of being addicted to an esoteric tradition requiring advanced scholarship, such an opinion is not supported by any direct proof. The average historian does not believe in the reality of a secret doctrine, therefore, he has no inclination to search for one. He is satisfied to assume that the cupidity of the Church and State accounts sufficiently for the extraordinary fanaticism which crushed the Templars.

In this work we are attempting to show that the Order of the Temple descended from the Secret Schools, and was a direct source of later esoteric Fraternities. We know, for example, that the German theologian, Johann Valentin Andreae, was a moving spirit in the universal reformation of mankind attempted in the opening years of the 17th century. We reproduce herewith the title page of Andreae's *Mythologiae Christianae,* published in 1619. The engraving is a mass of Masonic symbols, and includes one of the earliest representations of the combining of the compass and square now familiar to all Freemasons. At the bottom of this plate is the three-faced idol of the Templars represented exactly as it was originally described, partly bearded, and placed on a small base. We advance the speculation that this is a legitimate landmark connecting two important cycles of esoteric Brotherhoods. The other symbols decorating this remarkable engraving merely support those already mentioned. Worthy of note is the little figure in the circle on the left side of the design above the word *Grammatica.* Here a hand passes a human tongue to another hand, a graphic representation of the transference of a doctrine or "word." As we become sensitive to the pattern underlying the descent of mystical Fraternities, symbols originally obscure or unnoticed take on an obvious vitality.

Charlemagne and the Legend of Roland

Charles the Great (Charlemagne), King of the Franks and Holy Roman Emperor, was born in A. D. 742, and is remembered by popular historians for the brilliance of his reign, the success of his arms, the number of his wives, and

his diet of spitted venison. A considerable part of his life
was devoted to the extension and protection of his domains
and the quelling of rebellions among his subjects, but he
found time in the interludes between his military campaigns
to be the moving spirit in an important revival of arts and

CHARLEMAGNE
From an early illumination, preserved in the monastery of St. Calisto in Rome.

letters. He not only encouraged scholarship but practiced
it moderately himself, and is believed to have obtained some
proficiency in Latin grammar, rhetoric, dialectics, and
astronomy. Such intellectual accomplishments were unusual to royalty of the 8th century and resulted in a mini-

mum of grammatical errors in his edicts and legislations. It is probable that he could read and write, but he depended largely upon professional clerks for his extensive knowledge of history and religion. Like Akbar, the great Mogul who attained the distinction of being the world's most highly educated illiterate, Charlemagne found it more economical to hire readers than to burden his mind and time with too much schooling.

Although Charlemagne was crowned Emperor of the Holy Roman Empire by Pope Leo III, and was presented with the keys to the grave of St. Peter, he never was actually the sovereign of the Romans. His real position was that of protector and defender of the Popes. He encouraged a revision of the text of the Latin *Vulgate,* and left a considerable library of old manuscripts and records. He lived beyond his seventieth year and is said to have died of pleurisy. The historical Charlemagne became the central figure in an important cycle of myths and legends of profound interest to students of the esoteric tradition.

The Orders of Chivalry were dedicated to the restoration of the primitive Christian Church as it existed in the time of the apostles. In order to accomplish this restoration, it was necessary to rediscover the high secrets of the Christian Mysteries. The esoteric Association of the San Grael, the Knighthood of the Round Table, the Knights Templars, the Knights Hospitalers of St. John of Jerusalem, and the Teutonic Knights have been called "the military apostles of the religion of love." Heckethorn describes them as "military troubadours, who, under the standards of justice and right, fought against the monstrous abuses of the Theocratic regime, consoled the 'widow'—perhaps the Gnostic Church—protected the 'sons of the widow'—the followers of Manes—and overthrew giants and dragons, inquisitors and churchmen. The powerful voice of the furious Roland,

ORDERS OF THE QUEST 41

which made breaches in the granite rocks of the mountains, is the voice of that so-called heresy which found its way into Spain, thus anticipating the saying of Louis XIV, 'there are no longer any Pyrenees.' "*

In A. D. 778 Charlemagne invaded Spain, captured Pamplona, and laid siege to Saragossa. In the midst of his campaign, news reached the king of a revolt among his Saxon subjects, and he was forced to abandon the Spanish war and hasten back to the Rhine. Incidentally, perhaps the change in plans was not entirely unwelcome, for the siege of Saragossa was going badly. While withdrawing the main body of his army through the wild gorges and hazardous defiles of the Pyrenees, his rear guard was cut off and completely annihilated by the Basques. These mountaineers attained this signal victory by starting avalanches in narrow places along the road and hurling boulders down upon the Franks. Among the generals of Charlemagne's army who perished in this action was Hruodland, praefect of the Breton march. On this slight historical foundation was built the hero legend of Roland (Hruodland), one of the great epics of the Age of Chivalry. In its final form the *Chanson de Roland* bears little resemblance to sober fact, but it is an excellent example of the allegories ingeniously devised by the Troubadours for the perpetuation of their Mystery cult.

According to the legend of Roland, this culture hero is represented as the nephew of Charlemagne. He is one of the "twelve peers" forming the supreme council of the Frankish king. These peers, like the Knights of the Round Table, were nobles of exceptional valor and high integrity, all save one, the perfidious Lord Ganelon, whose treachery destroyed the sacred assembly. In the terms of this symbol-

---

*See *Secret Societies of All Ages*.

ism, Charlemagne, the initiated Christian king-emperor, represents Christ; his twelve peers are the apostles. Roland is John the Beloved, and Ganelon is Judas. Thus Charlemagne, the wise and righteous monarch, the glorious king and the preserver of the faith, like Solomon and Arthur, personify the Sun, and his peers, the twelve signs of the zodiac.

Roland is a Christian Siegfried, a form of the "hero of the world." In the legend of Roland, the Basques vanish entirely, and in their place is the vast army of the Saracens, the hosts of the unbelievers. The scene of the great battle is still the Pyrenees, and here the twelve peers, including Roland, Oliver, and the valiant Archbishop Turpin, the warrior-priest, die together to protect the withdrawal of Charlemagne and the main body of his army.

At the time of the actual battle, Charlemagne was only thirty-six years old, but in the legend he is represented as a venerable man with long white hair and beard. The treason of Ganelon is revealed to the king in a dream, and when from a distance he hears the last blasts of Roland's war trumpets he returns to save his beloved nephew, but arrives too late. In the story he "wreaks a terrible vengeance" upon the Saracens, but this has no foundation in fact. Lord Ganelon is tried for treason, found guilty, and torn to pieces by wild horses.

An interesting reference to the court of Prester John occurs in the legends of Roland. In this account, Roland, afflicted with madness, wandered in the wilderness. At the court of Charlemagne, the peers resolved to seek the stricken hero, and Astolpho, the poet-knight, declared that he would devote himself to the quest. By a happy accident, the winged horse of Atlantes had fallen into the keeping of Astolpho. Mounting the steed of high verse, the poet-knight flew beyond the regions of Ethiopia, and alighted in the wonderous realm of the mighty Prester John.

According to this legend, Prester John was unhappy because he had been unable to cross the great mountains to the spring of eternal life, where old age was unknown and to which death never came. When Prester John attempted to reach this spring, horrible disasters came upon the expedition, and a voice from heaven spoke: "Think not, vain man, to pry into the secret things of the Most High!" From that time on, the court of Prester John was afflicted by the presence of seven Harpies that screamed and howled in the air and snatched the food from the banquet tables. Astolpho, by the blast of his magic horn, dispersed the Harpies; and in gratitude, Prester John supplied a band of warriors to assist Astolpho in his search for Roland.

Although Charlemagne outwardly sustained the papacy, he was the Grand Master of a mystical and philosophical Fraternity which had descended from the Bards, the Druids, and the Drotts. As an initiate-king he is revealed as a patron of learning and the arts, and the virtual founder of the university system in Europe. He enriched the cloister schools, broadened their scope, and introduced many useful branches of secular instruction. His wars against the Saracens merely signified his victory over the subversive, antisocial forces of ignorance. Wagner, in his mystical music-drama, *Parsifal,* places the magical garden of Klingsor, the sorcerer, in a valley of Moorish Spain. In the original presentation of the opera, Klingsor was costumed as a Near Eastern potentate, and the flower maidens, whom he controlled by his enchantments, were dressed like the houris of *The Arabian Nights' Entertainment.* In recent years the Metropolitan Opera in New York has revived the correct costuming.

The earlier Orders of Chivalry practiced three degrees
or grades of initiation. Candidates first became pages, then
squires, and finally knights. After the mingling of the old
military Fraternities with such mystical sects as the Albigenses and the Ghibellines, the number of degrees was increased. In some groups there were as many as thirty-three
grades somewhat similar to the structure of modern Freemasonry. The romances of the Round Table, the Holy
Grail, and the Circle of Charlemagne certainly originated
in the esoteric teachings of the Nordic, Gothic, and Celtic
rites. Such legends as those of Parsifal, King of the Grail,
and the Swan-knight Lohengrin, his son, are veiled reports
of the Secret Schools of the adepts.

Wagner's interpretation of the Grail Cycle, though based
upon early traditions, was largely colored by his own
mystical convictions. As he glorified the Orders of Chivalry
in his Grail operas, so he dignified the guilds, which had
the same origin, in his *Meistersinger of Nuremberg*. The
knight-initiates of the Brotherhoods of the Quest performed
vigils, cultivated visions, and lived by rules and regulations
as rigid as any monastic Order. They had signs and passwords and were bound together by secret vows and obligations. They were dedicated to the protection of the weak,
the preservation of righteous peace, and the perpetuation
of certain spiritual and philosophical secrets.

When the Inquisition accused the Knights Templars of
worshiping demons and practicing obscene and abominable
rites, these accusations merely referred to the pagan doctrines held in secret by this Order of Chivalry. After the
destruction of the Templars, the esoteric tradition of Europe
disappeared from public view to be restated cautiously in
the curious terminology of the alchemists, the cabalists, the
Rosicrucians, and even the astrologers. The Orders of the

Quest gave place to the Orders of the Great Work. The elixir of life in the alchemical bottle is identical in meaning with the blood of Christ in the Holy Chalice. Even the dragons and monsters of the hero myths survived in the hieroglyphical drawings of the alchemistical philosophers.

Charlemagne with his twelve peers is Odin, the Grand Master of the Drotts, seated in council with the twelve Ases in the high and secret palace of Asgard. The brave Lord Roland is Tammuz, Dionysus, Sigurd, Balder, Sir Galahad, and Robin Hood. All these gallant champions of the human cause, these defenders of the weak, these princes of the Philosophic Empire, these soldiers of spiritual democracy personify the initiates of the Mystery Schools. The adept is the eternal "hero of the world."

The Troubadours

The Manichaeans, the neo-Manichaeans, and the post-Manichaeans went far afield to find grist for their mill. There was an old Druidic footing under the culture of the Gauls. One of the three branches of the Druid Order was known as the Bards. They were the wandering poets and minstrels, the singers of the Mysteries, concealing profound spiritual truths under gay songs, stories, fables, and myths. The Bards were a closely organized group. They had signs, words, and secret means of knowing each other. They had a sign of distress, which compelled others of their Order to come to their assistance in time of trouble. These wandering singers and storytellers played an important part in the social and ethical life of early Europe. They carried news from place to place, and, needless to say, the reports which filtered through the Bards took on a coloring appropriate to the problem of the moment. In this way, these poet-singers exercised a powerful religious, philosophical, and political influence.

The machinery of the Druidic Mysteries was revived by the descendants of the sons of Manes, to become the mechanism behind the Troubadours. Actually there was no break between the ancient Mysteries and the post-reformation revival of arts and sciences, which made possible the modern way of life. "Virgil," says W. F. C. Wigston, "takes up the lighted torch of Homer and hands it on to Dante, who passes it to the genius behind the Shakespeare mask."

The Troubadours were armed with one of the most important of all psychological formulas: If one would change the world, teach the young. They appointed themselves the tutors of chivalry, and were regarded as peculiarly equipped to endow youth with an appropriate cultural viewpoint. On the surface, their advice was simple, honest, and effective, and obviously above reproach. They taught, for example, that a genteel man always mended an open seam in his garment; this is more important than to patch a hole. A hole may indicate long wear, but an open seam represents carelessness. Incidentally, these reformers were careful to prevent any open "seams" in their own association. Another precious bit of advice was, in effect: It is not important that the rich dress well, but most important that the poor dress neatly; small means plus neatness equal character.

It may be inferred by the political consequences of their activities that the Troubadours did not limit themselves to a consideration of what the well-dressed young man should wear. Beneath the surface was the doctrine of the rights of man. The Order taught chivalry toward the weak, and emphasized that service for the common good was Nature's highest calling. From the Troubadours came many of those glorious myths and legends of the Age of Chivalry, the moral fables that right always conquers, and nobility of spirit is the only true nobility to which man can attain. A goodly number of our children's fairy tales were first sung by the Troubadours. Sometimes the original story is much older, but these minstrels found a way to adapt the legends to their own purposes.

The Troubadours flourished in Southern France, Italy, and Northern Spain between the 11th and 14th centuries. It is now established with certainty that these men, who numbered about four hundred, were members of a secret mystical or philosophical Fraternity, dedicated to the discovery of those powers of the mind and heart which must be cultivated and disseminated before it is possible to bring about a universal reformation of mankind.

In his most stimulating article, *Alchemy and the Holy Grail,* Harold Bayley writes: "Everyone has heard of the Troubadours, but it is not generally realized that they were heretics under the ban of the Church and driven hither and thither by that relentless antagonist. Their mission, Aroux tells us, was to redress the wrongs of Rome, to take up the defense of the weak and oppressed. They were also represented and celebrated as the true soldiers of the Christ, the exponents of celestial chivalry, and the champions of the poor, attacking under all their forms the monstrous abuses of the Priesthood. It is said that great numbers of the higher classes became Troubadours, wandering from Court to Court and castle to castle, spreading the doctrine of the organization for which they were acting as emissaries."*

In France the Troubadours were protected by the Albigenses, for the obvious reason that both groups held the same convictions and descended from the same source. The great rituals of the Troubadours were called the Courts

---

*See *Baconiana* (1907).

—From the *Melopoiae of Tritonius* (Augsburg, 1507)

APOLLO ON PARNASSUS

This curious woodcut, sometimes attributed to Durer, represents the deity surrounded by the Muses and other mythological characters. The symbolism includes all the emblems which occur a century later in connection with the Rosicrucians and the Society of the Unknown Philosophers.

of Love.   Here under the guise of a most elementary and material passion they preached the gospel of the divine love of God for man, and the human love which alone could bring the Brotherhood of humanity.   The Troubadours dedicated impassioned ballads to the fair lady of their hearts.   Only the initiates, however, knew that this lady was the Isis of Sais, the Sophia of the Gnosis, and the Diana of the Ephesians.

The body of the learned, which formed the secret council of the Order, was the custodian of an esoteric tradition that had descended from the Druidic, Egyptian, and Chaldean sages.   These minstrels concealed their knowledge from the profane, not because they desired a superiority for themselves, but for the sake of self-preservation.   The name *troubadour* means a "seeker after something that is hidden," and a minstrel is a minister or religious teacher.   But if the Troubadours worked quietly and industriously to further their doctrines, the adversaries were no less cunning.   The Church and State, aware that open rebellion threatened if the Troubadours were successful in setting up their great Court of Love (world democracy), quietly but relentlessly tore down each structure raised by the singing sages. To preserve the social *status in quo* the Inquisition was set up, and one by one the initiates of Manes were trapped on some pretext.   The real reason for their destruction was their political plotting against ecclesiastical and temporal autocracy.   Once again the "sons of the widow" perished at the stake or gibbet, or were broken on the rack.

It is said that Dante was a Troubadour, and when we examine the structure of the *Divine Comedy* the conviction grows.   St. Francis of Assisi is believed to have received his first inspiration to mystical devotion from the Courts of Love.   Among other important names associated with the Order are Richard the Lionhearted and the poet Petrarch.

The veiled lady of the Shakespearean sonnets and Dante's
Beatrice were not mortal women, but the Virgin of the
World, the secret Mother of the Mysteries. We may suspect
that Giordano Bruno, a martyr in the name of progress,
knew something of these Mysteries when he wrote in a
letter: "I am displeased with the bulk of mankind . . . and
am enamoured with one particular lady. 'Tis for her that
I am free in servitude, content in pain, rich in necessity,
and alive in death. . . . 'Tis for the love of true Wisdom
and by the studious admiration of this Mistress that I
fatigue, that I disquiet, that I torment myself." Even the
uninitiated can scarcely miss the implication.

The names of the principal Troubadours, from Guilhem
IX, Count of Poitiers, to Guiraut Riquier, can be traced
in any standard text on the subject. From the membership
we gain a reasonable comprehension of the stations and
abilities of these initiate-poets and singers. We can also
trace the survival of the Order in the Minnesingers, later
Meistersingers, of the Rhine. The principles of the Minnesang reached Germany from Provence, one of the last
strongholds of the Troubadours. The Minnesingers also
addressed their songs to a lady whose name must not be
spoken, but in whose service the gallant knight must pine
away in desperate poetic devotion. One of the greatest
of the Minnesingers, Rinemar of Alsace, was called "the
scholastic philosopher of unhappy love." Names change,
but the substance of the tradition is ever the same.

The name Pleiad, from Pleiades, was first bestowed in
Alexandria, that Egyptian city of initiates, scholars, and
libraries, upon seven tragic poets who flourished in the 3rd
century B. C. Later in French literature there is reference
to the Pleiad of Charlemagne, King of the Franks, also an
initiate. In the last quarter of the 16th century, the French
Pleiade, a group of seven poets, of whom Pierre de Ronsard

was the most celebrated, attempted the renovation and enlargement of language as a means of literature and art. Lord Bacon is believed to have been in contact with the French Pleiade, and has been referred to as the eighth star in the "constellation of the poets."

Let us not deceive ourselves with the delusion that these servants of the Muses gathered by accident or appeared upon the intellectual horizon merely to glisten for a night. The Pleiade inherited the unfinished labors of the Troubadours, as these in turn were rooted in the confederation of the Orphic poets.

Taliesin, the Initiate

In the days of the good King Arthur, Elphin, the son of Gwyddno, had been granted a weir, which is a fence of stakes set in a waterway to take fish. Elphin was slow of mind, and it seemed that his wit was so dull that his father could think of no other way in which the young man could make a living except by profiting from the salmon catch. When Elphin went the next day to inspect his new weir, he found a leathern bag hanging from one of the posts. Upon opening the bag, Elphin discovered within it a living infant of wondrous beauty who had been cast up by the waters. He named the baby Taliesin, in reference to his radiant brow.

Elphin did not know that the mother of Taliesin was Ceridwen, the goddess of the magic caldron, nor did he realize that the beautiful child had no other father but itself, for it was born through sorcery and enchantment. Ceridwen was resolved to slay her own son, but when he was born, she repented of her evil intent and placed him in a stream where some stranger would find him. Much of this story is reminiscent of the legend of Moses and his ark of bulrushes.

While Taliesin was still a small boy he was brought to
the palace of the king, where he could listen to the court
Bards and minstrels. He had already gained considerable
reputation as a poet and singer, but he sat quietly in a
corner. As the entertainers prepared to perform, however,
he cast a spell upon them so that they could only bow before
the king and make meaningless sounds. When the Bards
accused the child of causing the sorcery, the great king bade
him come forward and explain himself and his actions.
The song of Taliesin on this occasion is one of the most
remarkable poems in the philosophical literature of the
world. Thus sang the Bard:

"Primary chief bard am I to Elphin,
And my original country is the region of the summer stars;
Idno and Heinin called me Merddin,
At length every being will call me Taliesin.

"I was with my Lord in the highest sphere,
On the fall of Lucifer into the depths of hell;
I have borne a banner before Alexander;
I know the name of the stars from north to south.

"I was in Canaan when Absalon was slain,
I was in the court of Don before the birth of Gwydion.
I was in the place of the crucifixion of the merciful Son
     of God;
I have been three periods in the prison of Arianrod.

"I have been in Asia with Noah in the ark,
I have seen the destruction of Sodom and Gomorrah.
I have been in India when Roma was built.
I am now come here to the remnant of Troia.

"I have been with my Lord in the ass's manger,
I have strengthened Moses through the waters of Jordan;
I have been in the firmament with Mary Magdalene;
I have obtained the Muse from the cauldron of Ceridwen.

"I shall be until the day of doom on the face of the earth;
And it is not known whether my body is flesh or fish."*

Taliesin exists only as a name in the old history and literature of the Welsh. Many early songs and poems are attributed to him, but of the man himself nothing is known. It was not until the 16th century of the present era that even a mythical account of his life was compiled or invented. Of course it is possible that early and little-known legends were drawn upon, but it is equally possible that a story was manufactured to explain the writings attributed to this elusive Bard. In any case, Taliesin personifies the perfect initate of the later Druidic Mysteries. We use the word *later* because in most of his poems a strong Christian influence is present. He was the Christian Druid, accepting the new faith, but rejecting nothing of the old.

The pagan philosophers of Britain and Gaul found many parallels between their own doctrine and those imported by the Catholic priests. It was quite evident to the wise men of the oak trees that Jesus was a Druid. His life and teachings agreed exactly with the reports about their own initiates, and the first Christian missionaries were not entirely loath to capitalize upon these real or apparent similarities. As a result, it is hard to say whether the Druidic Order became a pagan school of Christian Mysteries or a Christian school of pagan Mysteries.

---

*From the abridgment by T. W. Rolleston in his *Myths and Legends of the Celtic Race.*

The Druids believed in metempsychosis, and Taliesin sang of his previous lives upon the earth in the same verses in which he paid homage to Christ. The Bards were so certain that they would be born again in the physical world that they lent money to be paid back in a future incarnation. Several such agreements are preserved in the British Museum. Pagan gods and Christian saints were honored together without the slightest hint of conflict, and such legends as those of the Holy Grail and Arthur's Round Table reveal the two systems in an indissoluble compound.

Perhaps the Druid initiates knew more about esoteric Christianity than regular churchgoers of today would like to admit. These ancient philosophers were not overly impressed by appearances, and they accepted it as a matter of course that a great religion was by necessity a science of human regeneration concealed under mystical symbols. They applied their own Golden Key to the keyhole of the Christian fables, and were not at all surprised to find that it fitted perfectly. It is doubtful if the missionaries of the Church were as generous, and it is equally doubtful if they ever even knew what was happening. They were too busy making converts to investigate the minds and hearts of those they were converting.

It is impossible to bind those who have unfolded their own internal spiritual faculties to arbitrary limitations imposed by any formal religious system. In all faiths, those truly wise perceive universal truths, and the more philosophical a system of belief, the more useful it is in interpreting other systems that are founded upon similar principles. In his introduction to *Barddas,* Rev. J. Williams Ab Ithel quotes the following: "And when we consider that the Gorsedd of the Bards was but a continuation, in the White Island, of the circular temples of patriarchal times, we may feel assured that it is among the ruins of

Bardism, or the religious system connected with the primitive temples, we may hope to discover, if at all, that Golden Key concealed and secured, which can open the mysteries, or esoteric doctrine, of ancient nations."

Taliesin was the Welsh Orpheus, for, like the Bard of Thrace, he charmed the whole world with his songs. He even descended into the underworld, and the dark land was filled with his music. Like Tuan mac Carell, the old Irish initiate of County Donegal, Taliesin remembered the many transformations (incarnations) through which he had passed, and he sang of the beginnings of life and the growths of men and the histories of his people, because he had the memory of the long-living in his own heart. According to the legends he did not die, but was again transformed. He grew old, and then "he became young again;" and when feebleness came upon him, he journeyed to the secret place to await the renewal of his body.

Merlin the Magician

Who was the mysterious Merlin, held prisoner in a house of air or mist, to finally vanish into the earth attended by nine Bards, and taking with him "The Thirteen Treasures of Britain?" It is quite in line with modern policy that recent scholars, after reviewing the legends and fables which surround this magician, should solemnly conclude that he is entirely mythological. It never seems to occur to this learned gentry that myths may have secret meanings, and should be examined in the light of the religions and philosophies in which they originate.

According to the most common account, Merlin was born of an Immaculate Conception during the reign of Vortigern, King of Britain, who ruled in the 5th century A. D. In a strange book entitled *Merlin, Surnamed Ambrosius,* published anonymously in London, in 1813,* it is reported "that he was conceived by the compression of a fantastical creature, without a body." His mother was a royal virgin,

MERLIN THE MAGICIAN

In this figure, Merlin is represented in the garb of a monk to emphasize his Christian baptism. In his lap is a book, on the open pages of which are the words: "The Red Dragon."

daughter of King Demetius. A similar account appears in that most curious work *Comte de Gabalis,* which was first printed in 1684. Here it is stated that the father of Merlin was an elemental spirit of the order of sylphs, and his

---

*Reprint of the edition of 1641, by Thomas Heywood.

mother a Christian nun. The place of Merlin's birth is not known, but it is generally supposed to have been in England or Wales. Charles W. Heckethorn, however, says he was born on the Island of Sena in Gaul, this being one of the last strongholds of the Druidic Mysteries.

Merlin was baptized hastily in order to preserve him against the occult circumstances of his own birth, but throughout life he combined in his person the humanity of his mother and the unearthly quality of his submundane

94. *Vter Pendragon* raigned
18 yeeres. 498.

THis King (by *Merlins* meanes, a skilfull man)
Igrene, the Duke of *Cornewals* Dutcheffe wan:
On her he got, (though illegittimate)
The Chriftian Worthy, *Arthur*, ftilde the Great.

Vter Pendragon *poyfoned by the* Saxons, *after he had reigned* 18. *yeeres.*

—From *A Memorial of Monarchs*
UTHER PENDRAGON

father. While still a small boy, Merlin was brought to the court of Vortigern, where he confounded the priestly astrologers and made several extraordinary predictions that later proved to be entirely accurate.

During the reign of Aurelius Ambrose, who succeeded Vortigern, Merlin is said to have brought the mighty stones of Stonehenge from Ireland to the plains of Salisbury in a single night. This monument had originally been set up in Africa, and had been conveyed to Ireland by unknown means at a remote time. Merlin delivered the stones in Wiltshire by a whirlwind, and placed them as they now stand over the graves of British lords slain through treachery. Certainly this report cannot be taken literally, but if we understand by the circle of ancient stones the symbol of a Lodge of Druid initiates, the legend immediately has meaning. The Romans did not invade Ireland, and the pagan Mysteries were practiced there long after they had been destroyed in Britain.

Merlin also served the next king, Uther Pendragon, whose name means the head of the dragon. He served Uther as counselor and magician through the seven years of his reign, and by his enchantment made possible the birth of the hero-king, Arthur, the Boar of Cornwall. Arthur was the son of Uther Pendragon and Igerna, Duchess of Cornwall. Much is made of the fact that the earliest historical records of King Arthur contain none of the mystical elements with which we are now familiar. There is no mention of the Holy Grail, the Round Table, or the magic sword Caliburn (Excalibur), which was fashioned in the land of the fairies. But the early legends do say that Merlin the Magician was with Arthur at his court at Caerleon-on-Usk, guiding the young king with wise counsel.

Some writers have attempted to solve the historical problems by assuming that both Merlin and Arthur were gods of an old Mystery cult. In this vein Lewis Spence writes: "It is plain that he [Arthur], like Osiris, is the god of a mystical cult who must periodically take a journey through the underworld, not only for the purpose of subduing its evil inhabitants, but of learning their secrets and passwords in order that the souls of the just, the perfected initiates, will be enabled to journey through that plane unharmed. . . . That Arthur and Osiris are indeed figures originating in a common source must be reasonably clear to the student of the myth. Druidism is only the cult of Osiris in another form, and Arthur seems to have a common origin with Ausar or Osiris."*

Unfortunately the facts are somewhat more complicated. The Osiris myth itself is but a fragment out of context, and can never be understood by those who assume that legends wander up and down the world willy-nilly, imposing themselves upon themselves in endless confusion. Certainly the Arthurian Cycle is part of the initiate tradition, but the key to it lies not in distant lands but in some deep hidden place within the structure of human consciousness.

Merlin, like all these mysterious mythological sages, is the secret doctrine itself, born of heaven and earth and locked within a house of glass—the sphere of illusion. He is not some old Cymric demigod under a new name, but a personification of an order of learning. In all probability there was a historical Merlin; perhaps several old Welsh Bards and soothsayers have been combined to form the legend. But the true life story of Merlin the man will never be known for it was never recorded. The Merlin of the myth is the adept, whose identity has been absorbed into the Universal Mystery of human regeneration. The Great School is personified in each of its initiates. This is why the heroes of all nations pass through the same experiences. There is only one experience that can lead to truth, and there is only one description appropriate to those who have accomplished the divine adventure. Of course, all esoteric biographies are perpetuated in symbolic form, for it is impossible to put into simple words those mysteries of the spirit that are not of this world.

---

*See *The Mysteries of Britain.*

There is a secret legend that Merlin's invisible father moved through the ethereal atmosphere in the form of a serpent. The archdruids of Britain and Gaul were the winged serpents, and their most sacred symbol was the serpent's egg, a symbol of both the universe and the Mystery School. The Immaculate Conception was the second birth from this philosophic egg or the womb of the Mysteries. The magician is the Master of illusion and the oracle of Nature. This priestly adept is the ruler over all the rulers of the world by divine right. In the case of Merlin, the adept brought the circle of the living stones to Salisbury, not the monolithic rocks that now strew its plain, but the Gorsedd, the throne of the revelation of the ancient ones of the earth. The Gorsedd of the Druids became the Round Table of King Arthur. There is no break in the mystical descent, for the young king takes the place of the old king— long live the king! At first it seems that the magical caldron of Ceridwen gave place to the Grail, and that the old pagan Mysteries faded away before the light of Christendom. But exactly the reverse was true. The ancient wisdom ensouled the new faith, and the Holy Grail became the caldron of Ceridwen.

Merlin sleeps in his glass tomb like the mysterious Father C. R. C. of the Rosy Cross, who is said to lie quickening in a womb of crystal. The dying King Arthur floats away to Avalon in a ship of glass. Each will return to life in his proper time, for he is not dead but sleeping. The sleeping hero is the adept-self locked within the mortal form of Nature, a form which appears to reveal everything and at the same time conceals everything. We look about us and nothing seems hidden, but so little is understood. We are all prisoners in a crystal sphere. The universe itself is the geometrical vault, the many-sided tomb, in which lies buried the "hero of the world" awaiting the resurrection.

In the Druidic rites of initiation the candidate was placed in a coffin as one dead, and after three degrees (symbolically days), he was restored to life and accepted into the communion of the reborn ones, the initiates. According to Caesar, the Druids would never commit to writing their secret knowledge about the universe and its laws. It was not necessary, for they perpetuated their esoteric doctrines through the songs and poems of their Bards. Whoever can read aright the myth of Merlin will understand the hidden place four-square in the Island of the Strong Door.

The Arthurian Cycle

Walter Map (Mapes), who died about 1209 at an advanced age, was the outstanding English literator and humorist at the court of King Henry II. From the meager records of his life, he seems to have been, at least indirectly, associated with the Troubadours. He is often referred to as an ecclesiastic and certainly held several benefices, but there is no direct record of his ordination. At one time, Map was clerk of the royal household and justice-itinerant. He studied in Paris, attended the Lateran council at Rome, and traveled extensively.

Although it is believed that Map was responsible for linking the legend of King Arthur with the Grail Cycle, cautious researchers are inclined to question the popular account. The justice-itinerant was a busy man, and it is quite possible that such lengthy and involved legends as *Lancelot, Mort Artus,* and the *Queste* were the productions of a group rather than an individual. It appears likely, however, that Walter Map was responsible for the transplanting of certain romances of chivalry from the Continent to the British Isles, and mingling them with the streams of English folklore.

The Arthurian Cycle begins with Merlin—Merlin the Wise, Merlin the Wild, Merlin the Bard, Merlin the Mad.

Dr. S. Humphreys Gurteen, in introducing the character of Merlin, writes: "In point of time, he appears upon the stage long before King Arthur, his famous exploits reaching back even to the reign of Vortigern. He also represents the *intellect* of the world as depicted in these poems, while Arthur represents simply its *physical force*. It is to the necromantic skill and wise counsels of Merlin that the King owes his birth, his crown, his order of Round Table knights, and his victories. It is Merlin who as Court prophet and councellor, predicts the grandest events in the life of his sovereign, and without whose advice no affair of moment is undertaken."*

When Arthur was born he was wrapped in cloth of gold, and in fulfillment of an oath made by his father, Uther, was taken to the gate of the castle, and given into the keeping of Merlin. Arthur did not appear again in the legend until Uther, on his death-bed, acknowledged his son and recommended him to the barons as their rightful king. When the proper time came, Merlin, by his magic, caused to appear in the Cathedral Church of London, before the high altar, a large stone with an anvil of steel upon it and a sword thrust into the anvil. Beneath in letters of gold was the inscription: *"Who so pulleth out this sword of this stone and anvile, is rightwise king borne of England."* Only Arthur could draw forth the sword, in this way proving his right to the succession.

We are reminded of Notung, the sword of the Volsungs, which Odin thrust into the oak, and which only Sigmund could draw from the tree. The sword trial represents the release of the will from bondage to the material elements, signified by the anvil and the stone. Parallels in other esoteric traditions indicate that the test of the sword symbolizes initiation.

*See *The Arthurian Epic* (New York and London, 1895).

Most interpreters of the Arthurian Cycle assume that it was devised by Bards and trouveres merely for the entertainment of high lords and ladies. Even those who acknowledge the possibility that the legends of Charlemagne

95. Arthur. 516.

OF the nine Worthies was this Worthy one,
　　Denmarke, and *Norway*, did obey his Throne:
In twelue set Battels he the *Saxons* beat,
Great, and to make his Victories more great,
The Faithlesse *Sarazens* he ouercame,
And made them honour high *Iehouah's* Name.
The Noble order of the *Table round*,
At *Winchester*, his first inuention found.
Whilst he beyond Sea fought to win Renowne,
His Nephew *Mordred* did vsurpe his Crowne,
But he return'd, and *Mordred* did confound,
And in the fight great *Arthur* got a wound,
That prou'd so mortall, that immortally
It made him liue, although it made him dye.
Full sixteene yeeres the Diadem he wore,
And euery day gaind Honour more and more.

Arthur the great was buried at Glastenbury.

—From *A Memorial of Monarchs*
KING ARTHUR

and his twelve paladins may have been transferred to the British clime have not sensed any serious purpose behind the circumstance. It is so easy to be deceived by the obvious, especially when the historian has no sympathy for the esoteric tradition. Arthur ruled over a court of heroes, much as Odin, the All-father of the Drotts, presided at the councils of the twelve Ases in the great court at Asgard.

King Arthur, like Siegfried, emerges as a type of the culture hero. As Hercules performed twelve labors, so

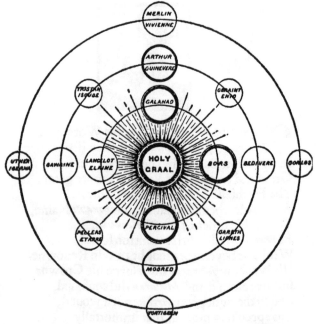

—From *The Arthurian Epic*

A diagrammatic arrangement of the Arthurian Epic Cyclus, according to the narrative of the Anglo-Norman trouveres.

Arthur fought twelve battles in the service of God and Britain. He was betrayed by one of his own trusted knights. As Odin perished with his Ases on the plain of Ragnarok, so Arthur and most of his knights fell at the battle of Camlan. With the hero perished his great Order of the Quest. The *Morte D'Arthur* describes the passing of the king and how his body was borne away to Avalon on a black ship.

Arthur was crowned King of Britain A. D. 516, and he died A. D. 542 in the forty-first year of his life. On the field of Camlan the forces of light and darkness perished together, and the whole story is a thinly veiled account of the fall of the pagan Mysteries.

Gurteen includes in his work a diagram of the Arthurian Epic Cyclus, according to the narrative of the Anglo-Norman trouveres. The figure is so important that we reproduce it herewith. The identification of Merlin with the intellect of the world is a simple and direct key to the Neoplatonism and Gnosticism underlying this entire cycle of legend symbolism. It will be seen from the diagram that an order of spiritual descent begins with Merlin, passes to Arthur, and is consummated in the maiden knight, Galahad. A parallel is found in the cycle of Grail kings, Titurel, Amfortis, and Parsifal, and in the Gothic descent of Odin, Sigmund, and Siegfried. Lancelot du Lac was the foster son of Vivienne, a nymph. She may be the same as the mysterious Lady of the Lake, who gave Arthur the sword Excalibur, which had been fashioned for him by Merlin in his subterranean forge. Lancelot, like Sigmund, was unable to accomplish the Quest of the Grail, because of his sin against the sanctity of marriage. Like Sigmund also, he became the father of a spiritual hero, in this case, Galahad.

We cannot examine in detail the entire cycle, but if we understand Merlin to be the world-mind, and Arthur the world-form, then Galahad becomes the world-soul, and the legend unfolds its cosmic content. Arthur himself never attempted the Quest of the Grail, but through his Knighthood of the Round Table, which Merlin had devised and over which the king presided as Grand Master, the accomplishment of the Grail Quest by four holy knights was possible. Thus the Round Table becomes the material universe itself, ruled by the demiurgus, the Greek Zeus, presiding over the circle of divinities, the twelve great gods of Olympus. Merlin is Kronos, and Galahad is Dionysus. In the esoteric hierarchy, Merlin is the secret doctrine,

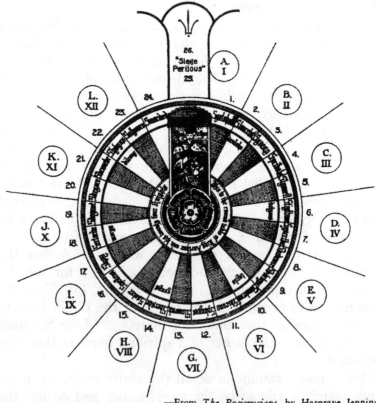

—From *The Rosicrucians*, by Hargrave Jennings
The Round Table of King Arthur, generally referred to as the Winchester table top.

Arthur, the formal structure of the Mystery Schools, and Galahad, the adept, in whose person the mystery of the redemption is revealed.

A table top supposed to be the Round Table of King Arthur is preserved in the courthouse in the castle at Winchester, and was reproduced by Hargrave Jennings in *The Rosicrucians, Their Rites and Mysteries.* Like most relics of the Mysteries, this table top is of unknown origin and uncertain descent. Jennings describes his drawing thus: "By tradition, the Round Table of King Arthur devolves from the very earliest period. The illustration . . . was copied from the original with great care and attention. King Arthur, in the principal seat, is idealized in the person of King Henry VIII, in whose time the Round Table is supposed to have been repaired and refaced. In the Revolution, Cromwell's soldiery, after the capture of Winchester, and in the fury at the imputed idea of *idolatry* (the Round Table is the English 'Palladium'), made a target of it. The marks of many balls are still conspicuous."

The center of the Winchester table top is ornamented with a large heraldic rose of the conventional form associated with the house of Tudor. There are places for twenty-four knights arranged in pairs, and a double throne for the Grand Master and the mysterious unknown knight, or adept, who is worthy to sit in the *Siege Perilous.* Like the tomb of Father C. R. C., Arthur's Round Table is a microcosm or mirror of the universe.

The knights met annually at Windsor, Winchester, Camelot, or Caerleon to celebrate the Pentecost. So exalted were these sanctified champions of the code of chivalry that not one could be given a seat above another. For this reason a circular table was constructed and dedicated to the Grail Quest. The table itself had magical powers and could enlarge its own size as the number of the virtuous increased.

The number of persons who could be seated at the table differs in the several accounts. One writer says fifteen hundred, another, one hundred fifty. The Winchester table seated twenty-six, but in the old records, the original table had space for thirty-two, including the throne of the king and the *Siege Perilous*. Thirty-two chairs plus the Grail throne in the middle would give the highly significant number thirty-three. Here is a possible Masonic intimation of thirty-two degrees earned and one bestowed by the "grace of God."

In one version of the legend, Merlin refers to the Round Table as the original board at which Jesus ate and drank with his disciples on the occasion of the Last Supper. Its mysteries were revived at the court of Uther Pendragon, from which it passed to Leodegrance, King of Cameliard. In the tradition preserved by Geoffrey of Monmouth, Arthur's queen, Guinevere, is described as a Roman lady, but she is usually referred to as a lady of Cornwall and daughter of King Leodegrance.

Arthur received the symbolic table on the occasion of his marriage, possibly as part of Guinevere's dowry. All the elements of the story have been intentionally or accidentally confused, but the implication is that the rites of the Round Table had descended directly from the celebration of the Pentecost by Joseph of Arimathea at Glastonbury.

Sir Modred, the Judas of the Round Table, was born of an illicit union of Arthur and his own half-sister, Morgause, Queen of Orknay. Arthur did not know that Morgause was of his own blood, but he atoned for his sin by dying at the hand of his wretched and evil offspring. Lancelot, who failed to stand beside his king-emperor at the battle of Camlan, finally died of a broken heart on Arthur's grave.

Although the historical Arthur was at best only a British prince, the legends make him conqueror of the world and finally master of the Roman Empire. Symbolically this is necessary, for Arthur personifies the lord of the material sphere. Materialism is finally destroyed by its own progeny, and of all the circle of the Round Table knights, Galahad alone not only attained the Grail but was translated to heaven without the mystery of death. From the birth of Sir Modred the same note of inevitable tragedy dominated the theme that hung over the Odinic Rites. As the body of the dying Arthur was borne away after the battle of Camlan, it was left for Sir Bedivere to perform the last rituals of the Round Table. He carried the sword Excalibur to the shores of the lake and threw it far out over the water. A hand rose from the deep and, grasping the blade, carried it beneath the waves. The sword is the power of the will, human and divine, which returns to space from whence it came in the day that is called "the twilight of the gods." Lord Tennyson then makes Sir Bedivere cry out:

> "But now the whole Round Table is dissolved
> Which was an image of the mighty world."

There are several accounts of the discovery of the grave of King Arthur. The most authentic of these records are those of Giraldus Cambrensis, who was present on the occasion, and William of Malmesbury, who lived at the time. When Henry II visited Wales, he learned from an ancient British Bard that King Arthur had been buried at Glastonbury, and that strange pyramid-monuments marked the grave. The king approached the monks of the abbey and further told them of a report that the remains of Arthur had been deeply interred, not in a stone tomb, but in a hollowed oak tree.

An excavation was made between two pyramids or columns standing in the cemetery of the abbey. Under a stone was found a leaden cross, which Giraldus says he actually held in his hands. The cross was inscribed with the words: *"Hic jacet sepultus inclytus Rex Arthurus in insula Avallonia"* (Here lies buried the renowned King Arthur in the island of Avallon). Beneath, at the depth of about sixteen feet, a coffin made of a hollowed oak was found and it contained bones of unusual size. Giraldus notes that the leg bone was three fingers longer than that of the tallest man present. The skull also was large and revealed the marks of ten wounds; nine of these had concreted, but the tenth, a large and clean cleft, apparently was the mortal blow. The remains of Guinevere were found on the same occasion, and also those of Modred, Arthur's son and slayer.

The bones were removed to the church at Glastonbury at the order of King Edward I, and were placed before the high altar. This king visited the abbey in 1276 and had the shrine of Arthur opened. After viewing the remains, Edward caused the bones to be folded into a magnificent shroud and had them replaced with deep reverence. According to one historian, the three bodies were buried in the same tomb, one above the other, with King Arthur beneath the other two. According to Thomas Gale,* Glastonbury was anciently surrounded by marshes and was called the Island of Avalon; that is, the island of apples, from the old British word *aval*. When Arthur was stricken by Modred on the field of Camlan, it is reported that he was carried to the Isle of Avalon to be healed of his wounds by Argante the Fair. Gale, quoting Matthew of Paris, says: "We do not know how he died; but as he is said to have been buried in the Abbey church of Glastonbury with an epitaph in this manner, so we believe him to remain there still, whence the line, *'Hic jacet Arthurus, Rex quondam, Rexque Futurus'* [Here lies Arthur, a King that was,

---

*See *Historiae Anglicanae Scriptores.*

and a King to be], for some of the race of the Britons believe that he will live again and restore them from a state of servitude to liberty."*

The epitaph supplies the last and most vital element in the compound of the culture hero. The "hero of the world" cannot die. He may retire to his tomb to sleep and to wait, but, like Charlemagne and Barbarossa, he will return to lead his people and re-establish the golden age. He is always identified with a glorious time long-past and a glorious time to come. The culture hero is the personification of the secret hopes and aspirations of the nation which invents him or bestows his qualities upon some historical personage. He is the immortal-mortal. He dies many times for his people, and yet, by enchantment, he forever lives. It will not require a great deal of reflection to discover in the legend of Arthur the conventional form of the adept tradition.

The story is finished. Long before, Merlin the Wise had been captured in the spell of Vivienne and no longer guarded the destiny of the Round Table. Out of the threads and remnants of this splendid mystery was fashioned the Order of the Garter (Guarder). In the Chapel of St. George, the knights of Christendom extended and overlapped their swords to form a brilliant star of gleaming steel. Once they had the Black Book, which told the secrets of the divine right of kings, but one day the book vanished from among them. This Black Book was the sacred writing of Hermes on the conduct of princes, the constitution of a united world. All that remains is the chain of the Garter, with its pendant of St. George the Dragon Slayer, the white and the red roses, and the motto, *Honi soit qui mal y pense* (Evil be to him who evil thinks), on a narrow band of ribbon.

---

*See *The Arthurian Epic*, by S. Humphreys Gurteen (New York and London, 1895).

Dante Alighieri

Gabriele Rossetti (1783-1854) was among the victims of the revolutionary changes in Italy. He fled from Naples, and settled in England, where he became Professor of the Italian Language and Literature in King's College, London. He was the father of Dante Gabriel Rossetti (1828-1882), English poet and pre-Raphaelite painter. Both father and son were enthusiastic Dantophilists, but it is the elder Rossetti whose contributions have the most direct bearing upon the descent of the esoteric tradition. The vast and varied lore which he brought to bear on the more recondite sense contained in the *Divina Commedia* and in the lyrics of Dante and his contemporaries will remain a memorial of literary labor and loving perseverance.*

Professor Rossetti was convinced that the poet Dante was a member of a Secret Society, and that his verses concealed a hidden meaning which had escaped the notice of earlier commentators or which they had intentionally ignored. The substance of his researches and the conclusions derived therefrom he published in London, 1832, under the title *Sullo Spirito antipapale che produsse la Riforma, etc.* Professor Rossetti includes Petrarch and Boccaccio among the number of the initiated Italians, but does not devote so much attention to their writings.

The researches of the elder Rossetti are of special interest when we realize that they were in print long before the concept of the descent of a secret doctrine through European schools of adepts had any prominent exponents or apologists. He therefore anticipated, by some fifty years, the convictions of the Theosophical Society and the schools of philosophical mysticism which emerged in the last quarter of the 19th century.

---

*See *Lon. Athen.* (1862, i.253).

It will be well to summarize the Rossetti hypothesis, even though his observations overlap, to some degree, material we have already advanced. To facilitate our ends, we shall also have recourse to *Remarks on the Disquisizion* (London, 1832), by Arthur Henry Hallam. A Secret Society, according to Rossetti, whose original is lost in the mysterious twilight of Oriental religion, has continued from the earliest historical point at which its workings can be traced to exercise an almost universal influence on the condition of the civilized world. These Mysteries, which in Egypt, in Persia, and even in Greece and Italy, preserved the speculations of the wise from the ears and tongues of an illiterate multitude, passed, with slight but necessary modifications, into the possession of the early Christian heretics. The Gnostic schools of Syria and Egypt transmitted to their successors, the Manichaeans, a scheme of discipline, which they perpetuated with extreme caution and in the most veiled language, as secrecy became more and more necessary because of the increased centralization of power in the orthodox prelates in Rome.

The Paulicians, whose opinions were for the most part Manichaean, preceded the more illustrious and more unfortunate Albigenses in a secret warfare against spiritual as well as temporal tyranny. The celebrated Order of Templars, so widely diffused throughout Europe, so considerable by the rank and influence of its members, did not differ from the Albigenses in the secret object of their endeavors or the more important part of their mysterious rites.

The rise of a new literature in the 11th and 12th centuries, explains Rossetti, afforded them a new weapon far more terrible than any they had hitherto employed, and capable of being directed to a thousand purposes of attack and

defense. . . . No path of literature has been untrodden by
these masked assailants. . . . In poetry, in romance, in history,
in science; everywhere we find traces of their presence.
Their influence, in some sphere or other, has been exerted
on all nations. . . . The love poems and Love Courts of
Provence and Toulouse were vehicles of political discussions,
of active conspiracy, and of heretical opinion.

The poet Dante was an initiate of this secret, political,
social, philosophical, and religious Society; a champion of
its means and ends. The proof is concealed in his *Vita
Nuova,* the *Divina Commedia* and its commentaries, in the
Convito, the *De Vulgari Eloquentia,* and others of his minor
works. Petrarch and Boccaccio were agents of the same
mysterious institution, and its rites and secrets can also be
discovered by those having the proper key to the confused
writings of Baron Emanuel Swedenborg.

Needless to say, the *Sullo Spirito,* etc. created a minor
tempest in the intellectual world. Arthur Hallam, speaking
for all the skeptics, pronounces the ideas which it contains
"interesting, ingenious, and impossible." Let us bear in mind,
however, that Professor Rossetti, himself a political exile,
was nourished from childhood upon the pabulum of Italian
socialistic idealism and secret assemblages. Both Petrarch
and Dante admired Arnaldo Daniello, one of the most
obscure of the Provencal poets. They called him the "great
Master of Love," but no one understood his songs, although
it is known that he was a Troubadour. It is impossible
to examine *Le Roman de la Rose* without realizing that
it refers to an esoteric Fraternity. The mystical import
of the rose symbol of the minstrels is certainly reflected in
the rose of Dante—the Rose Eternal "that spreads and
multiplies" in the Seventh Heaven, where the blessed
Beatrice is enthroned.

Mme. Blavatsky contributes some pertinent observations: "To genius alone it was permitted in those centuries of mental blindness, when the fear of the 'Holy Office' threw a thick veil over every cosmic and psychic truth, to reveal unimpeded some of the grandest truths of Initiations. Whence did Ariosto, in his *Orlando Furioso,* obtain his con-

—From *La Divina Commedia* (Firenze, 1892)
DANTE ALIGHIERI

ception of the valley of the Moon, where after our death we can find the ideas and images of all that exists on earth? How came Dante to imagine the many descriptions given in his *Inferno*—a new Johannine Apocalypse, a true Occult Revelation in verse—his visit and communion with the

Souls of the Seven Spheres? In poetry and satire every Occult truth has been welcomed—none has been recognized as serious."*

Dante Alighieri (1265-1321) was born in Florence of a respectable but not especially illustrious family. Little is known of his early life except that he met the little girl whom he called Beatrice when he was about ten years old, and she was in her ninth year. It has seemed reasonable to assume from Dante's poetic works and his letters that his infatuation for Beatrice (Bice Portimari) was the dominant personal emotion in his life. She selected Simone de Bardi for a husband, however, and died before reaching middle age. In 1292 Dante married, and the union was blessed with two sons and one or two daughters. Although Dante involved many of his acquaintances and enemies, at least indirectly, in his poems, no line or passage has been found which seems to allude to his wife. Beatrice remains to the end the mistress of his heart and soul.

For his involvements in the political conspiracies of the day, Dante was exiled from his beloved Florence, and spent the closing years of his life at Ravenna. He died of a fever, consoled by the mystical philosophy which had come to dominate his entire mind. Although Dante's fame is derived principally from his *Divina Commedia,* for our purposes the *Vita Nuova* links him most closely to the mystical speculations of the Troubadours.

The *Vita Nuova* explains how the poet, meeting Beatrice while still a child, concealed his true love [mystical adoration] by inventing a false love [human affection]. Later, after Beatrice had died, she appeared to him in a vision, persuading him to devote his life to study and reflection, thus proving his eternal devotion.

*See *The Secret Doctrine,* Vol. 3.

"We should certainly feel grateful," wrote Hallam, "for any theory that should satisfactorily explain the *Vita Nuova*. No one can have read that singular work, without having

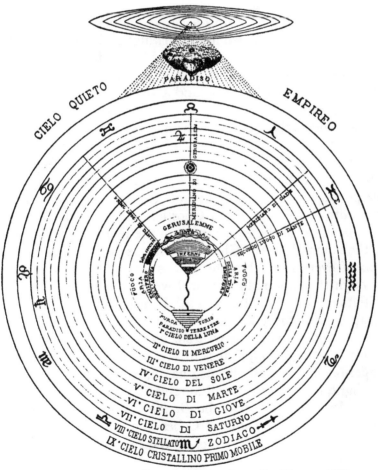

PARADISO

O FIGURA UNIVERSALE DELLA DIVINA COMMEDIA

—From *La Divina Commedia* (Firenze, 1892)

THE COSMOGONY OF DANTE'S *DIVINE COMEDY*

found its progress perpetually checked, and his pleasure impaired, by the occurrence of passages apparently unintelligible, or presenting only an unimportant meaning, in phrases the most laborious and involved. . . . Certainly, until Signor Rossetti suggested the idea, we never dreamed of looking for Ghibelline enigmas in a narrative apparently so remote from politics."

Let us compare Hallam's negative notions with the more positive attitude revealed in the writings of the distinguished Masonic scholar, General Albert Pike. He wrote nearly forty years after Professor Rossetti, and with all the lore of Freemasonry at his command arrived at almost identical conclusions:

"Commentaries and studies have been multiplied upon the *Divine Comedy,* the work of Dante, and yet no one, so far as we know has pointed out its especial character.[*] The work of the Ghibelline is a declaration of war against the papacy, by bold revelation of the Mysteries. The Epic of Dante is Johannite and Gnostic, an audacious application, like that of the Apocalypse, of the figures and numbers of the Kabalah to the Christian dogmas, and a secret negation of everything absolute in those dogmas. His journey through the supernatural world was accomplished like the initiation into the Mysteries of Eleusis and Thebes. He escapes from the gulf of Hell over the gate of which the sentence of despair was written, *by reversing the positions of his head and feet,* that is to say, *by accepting the direct opposite* of the Catholic dogma; and then he ascends to the light, by using the Devil himself as a monstrous ladder." Pike also points out that the *Divina Commedia* was based on the allegorical Table of Cebes and was the allegorical formula of the great secrets of the Society of the Roses-Croix.†

---

*Pike evidently was unaware of Rossetti's work.
†See *Morals and Dogmas.*

The primary difficulty that confronts the interpreters of Dante is the confusion caused by a historical and symbolical Beatrice. Unimaginative commentators cannot appreciate the entirely reasonable process of using an actual person to personify a spiritual truth. Yet Dante's personal acquaintance with the lady was slight, and his use of her in his mystical writings occurs only after her death. Certainly Dante did not intend to imply that he actually wandered about heaven and hell with Virgil as an all-sufficient guide. If the poet could involve himself in an allegory, why could he not also involve Beatrice? Nor is it more difficult to include Petrarch's passion for his mysterious Laura or Boccaccio's erotic devotions in the same category. We concede that the transcendental import of Boccaccio's *Decameron* is not immediately apparent, but neither are the true meanings of *Don Quixote de la Mancha* and *Gulliver's Travels.*

We agree with Bacon that he who cares for nothing but resemblances finds them in every hole and corner, and takes them on trust when he cannot find them. We must not build too much upon the uncertain foundation of coincidence, but, on the other hand, we cannot afford to overlook circumstantial evidence when it is present in sufficient amount. There can be no reasonable doubt that the mystical rose of Apuleius, the alchemical rose of Flamel, the Troubadour rose of Jean de Meung, and the cosmic rose of Dante grew on a single stem. Dante was certainly an initiate of the interior empire of the poets, and his allegories are no more fantastic than Trajano Boccalini's description of the universal reformation of mankind.

Beatrice is the Virgin of the World, and, like the dark lady of the Shakespearean sonnets, represents Eternal Truth for which all men pine away in hopeless adoration. Yet, inspired by this unattainable perfection, each embarks upon a knight-errantry of noble purpose. The fair maiden in distress, who must be rescued from giants, ogres, dragons, and tyrants, is humanity itself—the soul collective—victim of the conspiracies of Church and State. This is the simple part of the story. The program for the accomplishment of sacred and civil liberty was in the keeping of those initiates who had bound themselves with a secret and soul-consuming passion to the service of the veiled Virgin of the Mysteries.

—From *The Order of the Garter,* by Elias Ashmole

THE CHANCELLOR'S BADGE

The rose emblem of the Brotherhoods of the Quest is represented surrounded by the band of the Garter and the motto of the Order.

The Holy Grail

The Grail legends constitute a considerable body of mystical tradition. Although the accounts reveal certain common elements, the details indicate that a central theme was enlarged and embellished over an extended period of time. The Grail Cycle, as it has descended to us, originated among the Troubadours, the jongleurs, and the jesters. In England the Grail Quest became the central object of the Knights of the Round Table. The Arthurian Cycle in turn inspired the rituals of the Garter. This noble Order certainly belongs among esoteric Fraternities and Leagues of Chivalry, which perpetuated the secret doctrine of antiquity.

Elias Ashmole wrote an extensive history of the Garter, and was himself an officer of the Order. Referring to St. George, the patron of the Garter knights, Ashmole wrote: "It is recorded that King Arthur paid St. George, whose red cross is the badge of the Garter, the most particular honors; for he advanced his effigy in one of his banners, which was about two hundred years after his martyrdom, and very early for a country so remote from Cappadocia to have him in reverence and esteem." The reference to Cappadocia links the legend of St. George with the genealogy of the Grail Kings, for the Senaboriden originated in this region.

The St. George of the Garter is certainly the Perseus of Greek mythology who rescued the virgin, Andromeda, from a sea monster. Although the dragon episode is emphasized by Jacobus de Voragine in the *Golden Legend,* the actual life of the Saint is so obscure and uncertain that he is listed among those reverenced persons whose acts are known only to God. He seems to have been martyred in Palestine, and there is some evidence that two men of the same name have been involved in the popular tradition.

So great was the skill of the medieval storytellers and poets that their narratives have come to be accepted as fragments of a sober history. Several ancient communities claimed, for example, to possess the Holy Grail. It was supposed to have been in the keeping of the patriarch of Jerusalem in the 13th century, and the Christians of Constantinople, at about the same time, claimed that it was in their keeping. In the cathedral at Genoa, a green dish or vessel is preserved, which, according to the medieval Genoese, was the sacred cup. The vase or basin, which once contained the royal blood (Sangre Real), was supposed to have been carved from a gigantic emerald, which had once been the crest jewel of Lucifer. This glorious stone was struck from the helmet of the Prince of the Archangels by the sword of St. Michael, the champion of heaven, during the conflict which followed the revolt of the angels. The shining green stone fell into the abyss of outer space, where it remained until it was recovered by the angels and fashioned into the Holy Grail. The Emperor Napoleon I, a realist in matters religious, took the green vessel from Genoa to Paris, where he had it chemically tested. The highly-prized chalice proved to be green glass.

The legend of the heavenly emerald is reminiscent of the account of the Smaragdine Tablet, traditionally believed to have been discovered in the tomb of Hermes by Alexander the Great. Unfortunately, this Hermetic Emerald has proved as elusive as Lucifer's crest jewel, and sober reflection increases our admiration for the splendid inventions of the Troubadours. They were indeed universally learned, according to the measure of their times, for they drew upon a wealth of curious lore in the production of their wonderful and beautiful hero tales.

The legends were received with sympathetic understanding by the Bards and knightly Orders of Britain. In

the vale of Avalon in Somerset, Western England, stands
the ruins of Glastonbury Abbey. Here, according to the
songs of the gentle singers, Joseph of Arimathea nearly two
thousand years ago brought the holy chalice, which is now
said to lie buried beneath Glastonbury Tor. The Abbey
ruins represent the earliest Christian foundation in England.
The first church was a little wattled building believed to
have been erected by Joseph of Arimathea about A. D. 61.
The great church, later built upon the site, and all the
monastery buildings were destroyed by fire in A. D. 1184,
but rebuilding started immediately. In the year 1191 the
bodies of King Arthur and Queen Guinevere were found
on the south side of the Lady Chapel at Glastonbury. These
royal remains were later placed in a black marble tomb
close to the Abbey. This tomb survived until the 16th
century.

Around the legends of the Holy Grail in England were
developed the rituals, symbols, and emblems of the Order of
the Round Table. The circle of knights gathered about
the Table, which was the mirror of chivalry, representing
Jesus and his apostles at the Last Supper. There is nothing
to indicate in the epic of the Round Table that the questing
knights sought the Grail in the ruins of Glastonbury. Such
inconsistencies, however, only reveal the unhistorical dimensions of the legend. From the Arthurian assembly, the
Mysteries of the Grail kingdom passed to the Knights of
the Garter, whose Order represented the secret kingdom
of the heroes.

In a familiar form of the story, Joseph of Arimathea,
accompanied by a small retinue, reached England in the
1st century A. D. He brought with him the sister of
Veronica, who carried the napkin impressed with the
features of Christ. This napkin is the *Vera Icon,* the True
Representation, from which the name Veronica is derived.

In recent years, efforts have been made to prove that the plain silver cup used by Christ and his apostles in the celebration of the Last Supper is enclosed within the great Chalice of Antioch. This chalice, which was on exhibition in the House of Religion at the Century of Progress Exposition in Chicago, now rests in the vault of a bank in New York City. Thus it would appear that two cups are involved in the legend: one, the chalice of the sacrament, and the other, the vase of the sacred blood.

The Quest of the Holy Grail was the most important and most mysterious of the legends of the Orders of Chivalry. The knights of the Quest were supposed to be seeking a cup guarded by angels, which usually appeared to the pure of heart in a circle of splendid light and song, and veiled with a silken cloth. The blood of Christ, ever-flowing in the Grail, signified his true doctrine, and the cup which contained it was his Esoteric School, the chalice of his adepts. The search for the Grail was the spiritual adventure of regeneration, and the trials and tribulations of the knights concealed under veiled terms the story of initiation into the spiritual Mysteries of Christ.

As von Eschenbach reports the legends, the Grail was also a miraculous cup of replenishment. It yielded all manner of food and drink, and all who hungered after righteousness were sustained by its bounty. This account is all the more remarkable when the same mystic-poet states that the Grail was not a cup or vessel, but a stone. We may, then, think again of the Philosophers' Stone and the Hermetic Emerald. These several stories are fragments of one concept, and must be so considered.

We know that a division took place within the structure of the Christian communion at a very early date. The mystical sects, long-nourished by Diana, the great mother-goddess of the Ephesians, refused to accept the exoteric religion that rapidly laid claim to infallibility. Arthur Edward Waite wrote extensively on the Orders of the Quest. In one book* he attempted a survey of the entire field.

Harold Bayley, after pointing out numerous inconsistencies in Mr. Waite's approach, advances his own conclusions with considerable solid scholarship. The Hidden Church of the Grail was more than a mere pre-Reformation, Protestant motion; it was an esoteric Fraternity, a secular mystical communion, a conviction that the quest for truth was possible without benefit of clergy. This lodge of initiates, dedicated to the perpetuation of the universal religion and driven into obscurity by the dominant religious and political factions, existed secretly for many centuries subsequent to its disappearance from the sight of history.

Alfred Nutt, in his *Legends of the Holy Grail,* quotes Helinandus, whose opinions reflect the esoteric cult of the Grail, thus: "Christ Himself wrote the Book of the Holy Grail and save it naught else but the Lord's Prayer and the judgment on the woman taken in adultery." From this we may assume that the legends were held to be the most sacred tradition in Christendom and the true doctrine of Christ. It is not hard to understand that a dominant Church would oppose vigorously a sect claiming a spiritual authority superior to the apostolic succession.

Persecution, however, could not destroy completely the Secret Schools; rather it scattered the initiates, and in this way spread the very doctrines which it sought to eliminate. The bishops of the Grail Church had no distinguishing clerical habit, and between the 13th and 17th centuries, they were wanderers upon the face of the earth. Wherever

---

*See *The Hidden Church of the Holy Graal, its Legends and Symbolism considered in their Affinity with certain Mysteries of Initiation and other Traces of a Secret Tradition in Christian Times* (London, 1909).

they tarried they drew to themselves oppressed liberals and sowed the seeds of spiritual and secular liberty.

After the decline of chivalry, the initiates of the Grail Church made use of the guilds and the trade unions to disseminate their convictions. As times became more liberal, these survivors of an ancient faith found poetry, drama, literature, and music excellent means for spreading the gospel of an ideal human state. The confusion of modern living obscures the descent of traditions, but thoughtfulness will discover the facts. "The Glory of God," wrote Francis Bacon, "is to conceal a thing, but the glory of the king is to find it out."

The Grail Kings

It is difficult to formulate a brief statement of the origin of the Grail legend. Perhaps for practical purposes we may say that a philosopher and astrologer by the name of Flegetanis, while studying with the Arabs in their colleges at Toledo, compiled an account of the mysterious Grail. His records were discovered by Meister Guiot de Provins. This Guiot is the Kyot of the German version. Guiot was a jongleur, which was one of the grades or divisions of the Troubadours. It was from this jongleur, who was in Maniz in A. D. 1184, that the celebrated Troubadour and Knight Templar, Wolfram von Eschenbach, who died about A. D. 1220, derived the inspiration for his *Titurel*. He was followed by Albrecht von Scharfenberg, who wrote *Der Jungere Titurel* about A. D. 1270.

In the *Titurel* legends of Wolfram von Eschenbach, we have the source of the material used by Richard Wagner in the development of his Grail Cycle of music dramas. Of this circumstance, Harold Bayley writes: "If I were a believer in the theory of reincarnation, the spirit of a Troubadour Grail Knight reappeared, I should say, in the

HANS SACHS
Meistersinger of Nuremberg

person of Richard Wagner. The philosophy of Wagner was a remarkable blend of Catholic and Protestant, Christian and Buddhist ideas; it was curiously similar in this respect to the philosophy displayed in papermarks and wood blocks. Wagner appreciated that the highest and most potent mode of playing upon Humanity's heartstrings was by a combination of Music, Poetry and Stage-craft. His themes center around the mystery of the St. Grail and kindred myths. In his Mastersingers (The next inheritors of the Minnesingers or Troubadours) he gives us Hans Sachs, the historic cobbler-poet. In Sachs we see a representative of the unnumbered paper-poets, printer-poets and other artisans who combined work with aspiration. Sachs was a typical Son of the Dawn, one of those whom Bacon terms *Fillii Aurorae,* men 'full of towardness and hope.' "*

Although Hans Sachs served his apprenticeship as a shoemaker and practiced the trade throughout life, he had received a good education in Nuremberg, and traveled extensively among the German cities. He was a Lutheran, and selected literature as an avocation. He composed over 4000 *Meisterlieder* and some 2000 stories and plays. Sachs exercised considerable social and political influence, and Wagner introduced him in *Die Meistersinger* as a patron of intellectual and artistic freedom.

It is customary to assume, as pointed out by Dr. Karl Rosenkranz, that there are three distinct Grail traditions: the Titurel tradition which originated in Asia, the Parsifal tradition which is French, originating probably in Provence or Anjou, and the Lohengrin tradition which originated in Belgium. The history of Lohengrin, originally Garin-le-Loherain, is attributed to Hugo Metillus, who flourished

---

*See *A New Light on the Renaissance* (London, 1909).

about A. D. 1150. Thus all three stories or elements of the Grail saga can be traced to the areas where Albigensian communities flourished. It is said that Guiot, after contacting the Arabic records at Toledo, which had been written by a "heathen," searched all Europe for further details, which he could not discover until he examined the *Chronicle of Anjou*. It is all most mysterious and confusing, but the inevitable conclusion is that the Grail legends are intimately associated with the descent of Asiatic and North African mystical Societies through that period now referred to as the Dark Ages.

Several writers of the German school, with the thoroughness for which the intellectuals of that nation are justly famous, have studied the *Titurel* and *Der Jungere Titurel* in an effort to discover what may be described as the descent of the Grail kings. Their conclusions are most stimulating if we penetrate the outward pseudohistorical reports. It is immediately evident that the history of the Grail is the symbolical story of the descent of the Gnosis in Europe.

At the time the Roman Emperor Vespasian was laying siege to the city of Jerusalem, there was in his retinue Sennabor, Prince of Cappadocia, and his three sons: Parille, Azubar, and Sabbilar. Although Cappadocia was a Roman province, the root of the Senaboriden was in Asia. It should be noted that the names of these important Cappadocians had a distinctly Arabic flavor. Sennabor may be from the Arabic *senber,* meaning a *sage.*

After the fall of Jerusalem, the sons of Sennabor were entertained at Rome, and Parille was given the daughter of Vespasian in marriage. Her name was Argusilla, or Orgusille. Perille also received properties in France, and his brothers were given Anjou and Cornwall. To Parille and Argusilla a son named Titurisone was born, and he is referred to as the "stem of the Grail-race." Parille was poisoned when attempting to reform his people, and Tituri-sone became king. He married Elizabel of Arragonia, and their son was Titurel, the first of the Grail kings. Titurel, with the aid of the peoples of Provencal, Arles, and Lo-tharingia, conquered the heathen nations of Auvergene and Navarre, and had many wonderful adventures in the service of the true faith.

It was Titurel who was instructed by visions to build the temple for the preservation of the Holy Grail. The site was revealed to him by an angel, and so carefully hidden was this spot on the far side of the Pyrenees that none could discover it except by the aid of God. Like Odin's great Temple at Uppsala, the sacred shrine of Mont Salvat was built by miraculous means. By the grace of God, Titurel lived to great age and was four hundred years old when the Grail Temple was completed. The Divine Power then instructed him to marry and establish a royal line. The wife chosen for him was a holy maiden, by name Richonde, whose father was the king of a Spanish province. There were two children. The son, Frimutel, became the second Grail king, and he in turn had five children, the eldest being Amfortis, who succeeded his father in the royal line. Among the children also was a daughter, Herzeloide (the sorrowing heart), who was the mother of Parsifal. There was another daughter, Urepanse, who is referred to in the legend as the mother of Prester John.

Finally Titurel, having reached the age of nearly five hundred years, died in India, having warned both his son and his grandson that their lives would be filled with suffering because they had not conquered their human frailties. Parsifal was King of the Grail for ten years, and after the death of his son Lohengrin, who was murdered, he also returned to Asia. It is important to note that although the Wagnerian Mystery-dramas imply that the Grail legend belonged in the Age of Chivalry, the only available date in the earlier forms of the tradition is that of the death of Lohengrin, which took place approximately five hundred years after the birth of Christ. An excellent summary of this story is to be found in *Traces of a Hidden Tradition in Masonry and Medieval Mysticism*, by Isobel Cooper-Oakley. In order to develop the Asiatic phase of the story, it would be necessary to examine the records of the Nestorian Christians. This requires a complete program to estimate

—From *Peking*, by Abbe Favier

JOHN OF MOUNT CORVIN
Founder of the Catholic mission in China.

the degree that Nestorianism and Manichaeanism mingled their streams with those of Indian Buddhism.

While at first thought it seems remarkable that a Troubadour like Wolfram von Eschenbach should associate the Grail legend with Inner Asia, the circumstance is not so

strange as might appear. Christian missionaries of the
Syrian Church are believed to have reached China as early
as the 3rd century A. D. John Kesson of the British
Museum, in defining what he calls the second epoch in the
history of Christianity in China, writes: "We approach
the period when the Nestorian, or rather the Chaldean or
Syrian Christians, as they call themselves, spread so rapidly,
planting Christianity in the heart of Asia, carrying it to the
remotest East, and giving rise to the belief that they entered
the provinces of China early in the seventh century."*

Pope Nicholas IV in 1289 sent a Catholic mission, under
John of Mount Corvin, to the court of the great Mongol
Emperor, Kublai Khan. The Ka Khan was a sincere and
studious Buddhist, a patron of learning, and most tolerant
and considerate of the Mohammedan and Christian subjects within his domains. In a letter, Father John of Mount
Corvin, writing from the court of Kublai Khan, makes the
following rather significant statement: "A certain king of
these regions, George, of the sect of the Nestorians, who
belonged to the family of the great king who was called
Prestor John, attached himself to me the first year that
I was here, and, after he had been convinced by me of the
truth of the Catholic faith, was received into the *Ordines
Minores* and stood by me in royal vestments while I said
mass."

In 1338 a delegation of sixteen persons sent by the
Emperor of China arrived at the court of the Pope, who
was then throned at Avignon. The emperor asked for the
papal benediction, and further requested that the com-
mission be allowed to bring back horses and other rarities
of the West. Thus, although the Christian nations were
comparatively uninformed about the beliefs of Asia, many

---

*See *The Cross and the Dragon* (London, 1854).

Eastern sovereigns and princes possessed considerable information, even at an early time, about the life of Jesus and the rituals of Catholicism.

It would seem most unlikely that the Franciscan Father, John of Mount Corvin, manufactured the story of the Eastern king who was descended from the family of Prestor John. All the available records bearing upon the life of this good Father indicate that he was a man of the highest integrity. He further makes the simple statement that this king, whom he converted, was a Nestorian. If a Christian Empire existed in Asia at an early time, it must have been under the influence of the Nestorians, if not actually founded by them. We may ask why Titurel, the Grail king, journeyed to Asia when his time came to die? Also, why did Parsifal take the Grail to the Far East at the end of his own reign?

Nestorius, who flourished in the 5th century, was a victim of that same Cyril of Alexandria responsible for the martyrdom of Hypatia, the mathematician. Cyril accused Nestorius of heresy, and he was anathematized by a synod presided over by Cyril and one hundred fifty-nine bishops. The synod was declared invalid by the emperor, because the accused bishop and his friends were never permitted a hearing. Thus Nestorius was one of the early victims of the political machinery of the Western Church. It is believed that he was influenced by Gnosticism and the sect of Manes. It would be quite reasonable, therefore, that if the Grail kingdom, itself under the ban of the Church, sought refuge in a distant land, it would choose a location dominated by convictions similar to its own. The Nestorians, like the Albigensians, practiced a mystical communion and covenant outside the self-proclaimed Church of Christendom.

According to the earlist authorities, the Holy Grail was not only a cup or the sacred stone *Exillis,* but also was a mysterious gospel, a secret book. Eugene Aroux, the Catholic writer, favors this belief; and some have gone so far as to suggest that this book was the esoteric doctrine of the Templars and contributed to the Masonic tradition. It is evident that the story of Titurel and the symbolical genealogy of the Grail kings relate to the descent of Schools or Orders of initiates. Titurel represents the ancient wisdom and, like the mysterious Father C. R. C., is the personification of the Mystery Schools which serve the shrine of Eternal Truth. In the descent, the scene is gradually shifted from Jerusalem to Rome, and then from Rome to those areas in France which were the seats of the Albigenses.

Although these heretics were scattered by the Crusade against them, led by the Dominicans, their power was never completely broken. At a later date, another interesting and mysterious person appeared in Provence. He, too, left a strange legacy of poetic quatrains, and was the greatest prophet of the modern world. In the opening of his prophetic centuries, Michael Nostradamus describes himself as seated upon a tripod, like the priestess of ancient Delphi. His verses, which have never been completely interpreted, were written in the Provencal dialect.

To show that a body of lore continues through the centuries, extremely difficult to trace but linked definitely with the area under consideration, let us quote a few lines from a letter dated February 12, 1787, and addressed to a Theosophical-Masonic Society which met in Middle Temple, London. The letter was signed by Count Grabianka, one of the names assumed by Count Cagliostro. The letter is from "the Society at Avignon," and one section reads: "Yes, dear brethren, there exists a Society which the LORD JESUS CHRIST has formed. It was in the year 1779, and in the north of Europe, that he was pleased to lay the foundations thereof. Some of those who were first favored by his choice received afterward orders to go to the south. Five of this number being reunited, expected, for sometime past, their very dear brother GRABIANKA, etc. The rest, who are dispersed in different countries, earnestly expect the same order. We know already, that one of them, who has nearly finished his first course, will very soon join us. The ensuing spring will bring back fifteen, and we expect many more brethren and sisters that we know will be called in the course of this year."

Is it not curious that Cagliostro, the Grand Cophte of the Egyptian Rite of Freemasonry, should be associated with the Brotherhoods of Avignon? Is it not equally interesting that it should be generally acknowledged that the flamboyant Count was an agent of the surviving but elusive Knights Templars? To top this unusual sequence of events, it should be mentioned that the Lodge which Cagliostro visited in London was dedicated to the Swedenborgian Rite of Freemasonry, and that Cagliostro appeared among them claiming that the Secret Society in Avignon was practicing the esoteric Masonry of Emanuel Swedenborg. This industrious Masonic enterprise reminds us that in 1781 a Lodge of Masons was established in Paris for the purpose of uniting the Illuminism of Adam Weishaupt, the Bavarian esotericist, with the new mystical revelations of Swedenborg. The roster of this industrious Lodge included the names of Count Cagliostro, Anton Mesmer, and the Comte de St.-Germain. By this circumstance, St.-Germain is shown to be profoundly involved in the Bavarian Illuminati, the Asiatic brethren, and the Secret Societies of Avignon.

While the tradition may be confused and obscure, it is evident that we are confronted with the descent of a Secret School which existed from the beginning of the Christian era and formed an Esoteric Empire. This empire was known at one time as the Kingdom of the Grail, and was functioning as a political force in Europe as late as the rise of Napoleon I. Nearly every important transcendentalist of the last thousand years can be traced as being affiliated with this hidden empire. Research will fill in the few and inconsequential breaks in this golden chain of initiates, but the Temple on the three peaks of Salvaterra remains hidden unless it is revealed by the will of God.

Prestor John, the Phantom Emperor of the World

In the year A. D. 1144, Hugo, Bishop of Gabala, reported that a certain John, who governed as priest-king in an inaccessible region of the Far East, had, together with his people, been converted to Nestorianism. This John belonged to the race of the three Magi (adepts), and so extraordinary was his wealth that he carried a scepter of pure emeralds. In this way the rumor spread about Europe that a mysterious Christian monk was the supreme ruler over the nations of Asia. From some remote fastness of the trans-Himalaya, the power of this man extended throughout the three Indies. In 1165, kings and princes of Europe, including Barbarossa, received letters and long documents from the Emperor of the East. In these epistles, the writer described himself as John the Presbyter, Priest of the Almighty Power of God and of Our Lord Jesus Christ. One of these letters to his friend, Manuel, Prince of Constantinople, opened with the words, "I, Prester John, the Lord of Lords, surpass all under heaven in virtue, in riches, and in power. . . ."

In this document, Prestor John devoted considerable space to the description of his empire. Among other curious notes, he describes monstrous ants that dug gold out of the earth, and fish from whose bodies might be extracted imperishable purple dyes. There were also pebbles which gave forth light, restored the sight of the blind, and ren-

—From *Ho Preste Joam Das Indias* (Lisbon, 1540)

PRESTOR JOHN AS EMPEROR OF ETHIOPIA

dered the possessor invisible. Here flowed the Fountain of
Youth, and there was a sea of sand in which swam
a strange kind of fish. Here, also, was the home of the
salamander, a worm which lived in fire, and from whose

wool were woven the incombustible garments of the king, which were washed by flames. (Salamander's wool is the ancient name for asbestos.)

In the land of Prester John, there was no poverty, no crime, and no vice. Before his palace, which was splendid beyond description, was a magic mirror by which the emperor could see throughout his dominions and detect all conspiracy against the State. He was constantly waited upon by seven kings, sixty dukes, and three hundred sixty-five counts. Twelve archbishops sat at his right hand and twenty bishops at his left. Yet, with all this grandeur, he was a modest and humble man who did not rejoice in worldly splendor, and chose only to be called Presbyter, even though his butler was an archbishop, his chamberlain was a bishop, and his chief cook was a king.

Early travelers to the Far East brought back lurid accounts of this strange monarch, who maintained a standing army of a million and a half warriors, and was complete master of the birthplace of the sun. Even Marco Polo returned with an extravagant story of a Christian Emperor of Tibet, whose colonies included Persia, Ceylon, and Siam, and whose powers were limitless. It is impossible to dismiss the story of Prester John as a mere fable, for legendary men do not write letters or send embassies. On the other hand, no account of this strange man is to be found in Oriental histories, which were amazingly comprehensive.

Wolfram von Eschenbach was the most important of the medieval German poets, and was a Minnesinger. In his epic poem, *Parzifal,* he connected for the first time the legend of the Holy Grail with the history of Prester John. Parsifal, the mythical King of the Holy Grail, carried the sacred cup to Asia, where he received the name of Prester John. Thus we see that the Secret Orders of Europe were involved in the perpetuation of the curious fable of the Asiatic Lord of Lords.

After the era of exploration, by which the boundaries and proportions of countries came to be known with greater accuracy, the location of Prester John's empire shifted from one inaccessible area to another, and finally was identified with Abyssinia. At the beginning of the 15th century, the Abyssinian-Christian priests described their kingdom as the land of Prester John. This story gained immediate popularity, and the princes of Europe sent ambassadors in search of him. Unfortunately, these men were never heard of again. The Negus of Abyssinia combined in his person certain temporal and spiritual powers, and the name of John occurs frequently in the list of the Abyssinian kings. This entire theory, however, was finally abandoned.

The oldest map on which America is mentioned, dated 1507, placed the country of John the Presbyter in the area of Tibet. The following description appeared: "This is the land of the good King and lord, known as Prester John, lord of all Eastern and Southern India, lord of all the kings of India, in whose mountains are found all kinds of precious stones."*

In the first hundred years after the invention of printing, several books were published showing pictures of Prester John in his royal robes. Because of the lack of geographical data, many believed the boundaries of Abyssinia to extend to China. In fact, the discovery of the Cape of Good Hope was due principally to the efforts of the King of Portugal to communicate with Prester John. The long, sad story of the search for the phantom emperor can be studied at length in *The Land of Prester John, a Chronicle of Portuguese Exploration,* by Elaine Sanceau.

---

*See *The Catholic Encyclopedia* (article, Prestor John).

Most writers who have examined the tradition about Prester John have overlooked the one source from which they might have secured the real key to the mystery. Heckethorn was working in the right direction when he pointed out that the legend originated in the resemblance between Buddhism and Christianity. He explains that there was in China in the 12th century a great Mongol tribe professing Buddhism, which, by travelers, was mistaken for an Oriental-Christian religion. The Nestorian-Christians dwelling among the Mongols called the head of this Buddhist sect "John the Priest," and hence arose the tradition that in the heart of Asia there was a Christian Church, whose Pope bore the title of Prester John.

The original location given for the empire of Prester John was the area of the Gobi Desert, where he lived in an enchanted palace in the mountains. If you ask Eastern initiates to describe the Northern Paradise, called Dejung or Shambhala, the mysterious city of the adepts, they will tell you that it is in the heart of the Gobi Desert. In the old sand of Shamo, the Ancient Mother, stands the Temple of the Invisible Government of the World. High in the etheric atmosphere of the planet it floats, supported upon an outcropping of azoic rock, called the Sacred or Imperishable Island.

The fabled mahatmas of Asia should not be regarded as isolated initiates but as members of an exalted Fraternity, which has been called the Trans-Himalayan Brotherhood. This order of exalted men, servants of the Lord of the World, are the spiritual governors of the mundane sphere. They gather at prescribed intervals in the Temple of Shambhala on the Sacred Island and give allegiance to the Lord of Lords, the King of Kings, Regent of the Sun, and Master of the World.

That we are dealing with a cosmic myth and a story of the Esoteric Schools is evident, when we remember the seven kings (planets), twelve archbishops (signs of the zodiac), and three hundred sixty-five counts (days of the year), and other obviously symbolical numbers. Eschenbach realized this, for the Order of the Holy Grail, with its temple and its knights, is only a veiled reference to Shambhala. It seems that the Invisible Government was involved in the crisis caused by the rise of Genghis Khan. It never occurred to the Christian historians that the Sacred City of the gods could be anything except an Asiatic version of Rome. Beneath the name and legend of Prester John is concealed the identity of the unknown and unnamed thirteenth and highest adept of the Philosophic Empire. Naturally, he could not be found, but the Golden City sought by the Portuguese is the same abode of the god-men that Lao-tse was seeking when he departed alone into the sand of Shamo, riding on his green ox.

Printed in the USA
CPSIA information can be obtained
at www.ICGtesting.com
LVHW041153010924
789848LV00026B/551